Ending the Crisis of Capitalism or Ending Capitalism?

Through the voices of the peoples of Africa and the global South, Pambazuka Press and Pambazuka News disseminate analysis and debate on the struggle for freedom and justice.

Pambazuka Press – www.pambazukapress.org

A Pan-African publisher of progressive books and DVDs on Africa and the global South that aim to stimulate discussion, analysis and engagement. Our publications address issues of human rights, social justice, advocacy, the politics of aid, development and international finance, women's rights, emerging powers and activism. They are primarily written by well-known African academics and activists. All books are available as ebooks.

Pambazuka News – www.pambazuka.org

The award-winning and influential electronic weekly newsletter providing a platform for progressive Pan-African perspectives on politics, development and global affairs. With more than 2,500 contributors across the continent and a readership of more than 660,000, Pambazuka News has become the indispensable source of authentic voices of Africa's social analysts and activists.

Pambazuka Press and Pambazuka News are published by Fahamu (www.fahamu.org)

Ending the Crisis of Capitalism or Ending Capitalism?

Samir Amin

Translated by
Victoria Bawtree

An imprint of Fahamu

This English edition first published 2011 by Pambazuka Press,
an imprint of Fahamu
Cape Town, Dakar, Nairobi and Oxford
www.pambazukapress.org   www.fahamubooks.org   www.pambazuka.org

CODESRIA
Dakar
www.codesria.org
and
Books *for* Change,
Bangalore
www.booksforchange.info

Fahamu, 2nd floor, 51 Cornmarket Street, Oxford OX1 3HA, UK
Fahamu Kenya, PO Box 47158, 00100 GPO, Nairobi, Kenya
Fahamu Senegal, 9 Cité Sonatel 2, POB 25021, Dakar-Fann, Dakar, Senegal
Fahamu South Africa, c/o 19 Nerina Crescent, Fish Hoek,
7975 Cape Town, South Africa

CODESRIA, Avenue Cheikh Anta Diop X Canal IV, BP 3304, CP 18524,
Dakar, Senegal

Books *for* Change, 139 Richmond Road, Bangalore 560 025, India

French edition *La crise: Sortir de la crise du capitalisme ou sortir du capitalisme en crise* first published 2009 by Le Temps des Cerises

Copyright © Samir Amin 2011
The right of Samir Amin to be identified as the author of this work
has been asserted by him in accordance with the Copyright,
Designs and Patents Act 1988.

All rights reserved. Redistribution of the material presented in this work
is encouraged by the publisher, provided that the original text is not altered,
that the original source is properly and fully acknowledged and that the
objective of the redistribution is not commercial gain. Please contact
the publisher if you wish to reproduce, redistribute or transmit, in
any form or by any means, this work or any portion thereof.

British Library Cataloguing in Publication Data
A catalogue record for this book is available from the British Library

ISBN: 978-1-906387-80-8 paperback
ISBN: 978-1-906387-83-9 ebook – pdf
ISBN India: 978-81-8291-109-3

Printed by National Printing Press, Bangalore, India

Contents

Translator's note		vi
Introduction		1
1	The financial collapse of liberal globalisation	21
2	The contrast between the European and the Chinese historical developments	40
3	Historical capitalism – accumulation by dispossession	51
4	Revolutionary advances and catastrophic retreats	78
5	Peasant agriculture and modern family agriculture	101
6	Humanitarianism or the internationalism of the peoples?	129
7	Being Marxist, being communist, being internationalist	146
Index		195

Translator's note

I feel it might be helpful to clarify some of the words and phrases in this book which, because they refer to specifically French phenomena, cannot be translated without distorting the meaning. For example 'bobo', a term widely used in French newspapers and journals in recent years, signifies 'bohemian bourgeois' and it refers, in the words of the author of this book, to those of the upper middle classes who lean to the left as long as their privileges are maintained. Of course 'champagne socialists' gives the idea but it somehow limits the term to those who get together for expensive eating and drinking, while proclaiming themselves to be of the left. Bobo is a rather deeper concept and refers to more general political and social behaviour.

Then there is the phrase 'actually existing socialism' (and, by extension, though less often, 'actually existing capitalism' or even 'actually existing globalisation'). It came to be used several decades ago by independent thinkers on the left who, while advocating socialism, felt the need to distance themselves from the 'socialist' societies in Eastern Europe, set up under the domination of the Soviet Union. In the minds of people like Ernest Mandel and Rudolf Bahro these societies were in many ways a travesty of socialism.

Samir Amin often uses the French word *'dérive'*, referring to the way in which principles or policies gradually lose their impetus and end up in positions quite contrary to their original purpose. Sometimes this is a deliberate decision on the part of a group or party but in any case the process is usually slow (and often unrecognised), hence the word *'dérive'*, which seems to me to be best translated as 'drift'.

The author uses the word *'representation'* not to refer to a theatrical performance or in the sense of an agent, but as Marx used it to describe the way in which a system presents itself to the members of its society in such a way that is convenient for those who dominate society but still convincing enough to obtain the consent of the dominated (if only tacit) if the system is to work. See particularly the section headed 'The Liberal Virus' in Chapter 7.

Then there are words which have different connotations in

TRANSLATOR'S NOTE

English and French. One of them is *'populaire'*, which cannot normally be translated by 'popular' in English, which generally means pleasing to the people at large, while in French it usually refers to the populace, the working and/or the under classes. This is the sense in which we use 'the popular classes' for lack of a better adjective.

Another such word is 'vulgar', which in English invariably means gross, tasteless, loutish. *'Vulgaire'* in French more often means ordinary, widespread or banal. This is the sense in which Samir Amin uses it when he refers to conventional economics, which, for so many years of his life he has been at pains to try and demolish.

Victoria Bawtree

Introduction

Capitalism, a parenthesis in history

The principle of endless accumulation that defines capitalism is synonymous with exponential growth and the latter, like cancer, leads to death. John Stuart Mill, who recognised this, imagined that a stationary state of affairs would put an end to this irrational process. John Maynard Keynes shared this optimism of reason. But neither was equipped to understand how the necessary overcoming of capitalism could prevail. By contrast, Marx, by giving proper importance to the new class struggle, could imagine the reversal of the power of the capitalist class, concentrated nowadays in the hands of the ruling oligarchy.

Accumulation, which is synonymous with pauperisation, provides the objective framework of the struggles against capitalism. But accumulation expresses itself mainly through the growing contrast between the affluence of the societies in the centre of the world system, who benefit from the imperialist rent,[1] and the misery of the societies at the dominated peripheries. This conflict becomes, therefore, the central axis of the alternative between socialism and barbarism.

Historically, actually existing capitalism (see Translator's note) is associated with successive forms of accumulation by dispossession, not only at the beginning (primitive accumulation) but also at each stage of the unfolding of the capitalist system. Once properly constituted, this Atlantic capitalism sought to conquer the world and has remade it on the basis of permanent dispossession of the conquered regions, which through this process became the dominated peripheries of the system.

This victorious globalisation has turned out to be unable to impose itself in a durable manner. Just about half a century after its triumph (which appeared to inaugurate the end of history), this model was questioned by the revolution of the Russian semi-periphery and the (victorious) liberation struggles in Asia and Africa which constitute the history of the 20th century – the first wave of struggles in favour of the emancipation of the workers and the peoples.

Accumulation by dispossession continues before our eyes in the late modern capitalism of the contemporary oligopolies. In the centres, monopoly rents – whose beneficiaries are the oligopolistic plutocracies – are synonymous with the dispossession of the entire productive basis of society. In the peripheries, this pauperising dispossession manifests itself in the expropriation of the peasantry and the plundering of the natural resources of the regions in question. Both these practices constitute the essential pillars of the expansion strategies of the oligopolies' late capitalism.

In this context, I situate the new agrarian question at the heart of the challenge for the 21st century. The dispossession of the peasantry (in Asia, Africa and Latin America) is the major contemporary form of the tendency towards pauperisation (in the sense which Marx ascribed to this law), linked to accumulation. Its implementation cannot be dissociated from the strategies of imperialist rent-seeking and rent-capturing by the oligopolies, with or without agrofuels. I deduce from this that the development of the struggles in the peasant societies of the South (almost half of humankind) and the responses to these struggles will largely determine the capacity or otherwise of the workers and the peoples to progress on the road to constructing an authentic civilisation, liberated from the domination of capital. I do not see any name for this other than socialism.

The plundering of the South's natural resources, which is demanded by the pursuit of the model of wasteful consumption to the exclusive benefit of the North's affluent societies, destroys any prospect of development worthy of this name for their peoples and therefore constitutes the other face of pauperisation on a worldwide scale. In this spirit, the energy crisis is neither the product of the growing scarcity of certain resources necessary for production (oil, obviously) nor the outcome of the destructive effects of the energy-devouring forms of production and consumption that are currently in place. This description, while not wrong in itself, fails to go beyond banal and immediate evidence. The energy crisis is the product of the will of oligopolies and a collective imperialism to secure a monopoly of access to the planet's natural resources, whether these be scarce or not, in such a way as to appropriate the imperialist rent. It would make no difference if the utilisation of these resources remains the same as it is now (wasteful and energy-devouring) or if it were subject to environmentally friendly measures and new correctives. I deduce from this that the pursuit of the expansionist strategy of the late capitalism of oligopolies will inevitably clash with the growing resistance of the nations of the South.

The current crisis is therefore neither a financial crisis nor the sum of multiple systemic crises, but the crisis of the imperialist capitalism of oligopolies whose exclusive and supreme power risks being questioned once more by the struggles of the entire popular classes (see Translator's note) and the nations in the dominated peripheries, even if they appear to be emerging markets. This crisis is also simultaneously a crisis of US hegemony. The following phenomena are inextricably linked to one another: the capitalism of oligopolies, the political power of oligarchies, barbarous globalisation, financialisation, US hegemony, the militarisation of the way globalisation is operated in the service of oligopolies, the decline of democracy, the plundering of the planet's resources and the abandoning of development for the South.

The real challenge is therefore as follows: will these struggles manage to converge in order to pave the long way – or ways – towards the transition to world socialism? Or will these struggles remain separate from one another, or will they even clash with each other and therefore become ineffective, leaving the initiative with the capital of the oligopolies?

From one long crisis to another

The financial meltdown in September 2008 probably took by surprise the conventional economists who advocated happy globalisation and threw into disarray some of the fabricators of liberal discourse, who had been triumphant since the fall of the Berlin Wall. If, however, this event did not surprise me – I expected it (without of course predicting its date, like some astrologist) – it is simply because for me this event is part of the unfolding of the long crisis of an ageing capitalism, begun in the 1970s.

It is good to return to the first long crisis of capitalism which fashioned the 20th century, as the parallels between the stages of the unfolding of both crises are so striking.

ENDING THE CRISIS OF CAPITALISM OR ENDING CAPITALISM?

The industrial capitalism that was triumphant in the 19th century entered a crisis from 1873 onwards. Profit rates dropped, for the reasons highlighted by Marx. Capital reacted with a double move: concentration and globalised expansion. The new monopolies confiscated in addition to their profits a rent levied on the massive added value generated by the exploitation of labour. They reinforced the colonial conquests of the planet. These structural transformations allowed a new surge in profits. These transformations led to the belle époque – from 1890 to 1914 – which is the period of globalised domination by financial monopoly capital. The dominant discourses of the time praised colonisation (its civilising mission) and described globalisation as synonymous with peace, and the workers' social democracy rallied to the cause.

However, the belle époque, announced as the end of history by the ideologues of this period, ended in the First World War, as only Lenin had predicted. And the period which followed and lasted until the aftermath of the Second World War was the period of wars and revolutions. In 1920, after the Russian Revolution (the weak link in the system) had been isolated following the defeat of the hopes of revolution in central Europe, the capital of the financialised monopolies restored, against all the odds, the system of the belle époque; a restoration, denounced by Keynes at the time, which was at the origin of the financial collapse of 1929 and the Great Depression to which it led and which lasted until the beginning of the Second World War.

The long 20th century – 1873–1990 – is therefore the century of both the deployment of the first systemic and profound crisis of ageing capitalism (to the point where Lenin thought that this capitalism of monopolies constituted the supreme phase of capitalism) and that of the first triumphant wave of anti-capitalist revolutions (Russia, China) and of the anti-imperialist movements of Asia and Africa.

The second systemic crisis of capitalism began in 1971, with the abandoning of the gold convertibility of the dollar, almost exactly a century after the commencement of the first crisis. Profit rates, investment levels and growth rates all collapsed (and never again reverted to the levels of the period 1945–75). Capital responded to the challenge, as in the previous crisis, with a double movement of concentration and globalisation. In this way, capital established structures that defined the second belle époque (1990–2008) of financialised globalisation, allowing oligopolistic groups to levy their monopoly rent. The same discourse accompanied this process: the market guarantees prosperity, democracy and peace; it is the end of history. The same rallying occurred, this time by European socialists to the new liberalism. However, this new belle époque was from the outset accompanied by war, the war of the North versus the South, started in 1990. Just as the first financialised globalisation had led to 1929, so the second produced 2008. Today we have reached this crucial moment which announces the probability of a new wave of wars and revolutions. The chances of this are even greater since the ruling powers do not envisage anything other than the restoration of the system as it was before the financial meltdown.

The analogy between the unfolding of these long, systemic crises of ageing capitalism is striking. There are, nonetheless, differences whose political significance is important.

A systemic rather than just a financial crisis

Behind the financial crisis, there exists a systemic crisis of the capitalism of oligopolies.

Contemporary capitalism is first and foremost a capitalism of oligopolies in the full sense of the term (which so far capitalism has only been in part). What I mean by this is that the oligopolies alone command the production of the economic system in its entirety. They are financialised in the sense that they alone have access to capital markets. This financialisation grants the monetary and financial market – their market, on which they compete with each other – the status of dominant market, which in turn fashions and commands the labour and commodity exchange markets.

This globalised financialisation expresses itself by a transformation of the ruling bourgeois class, which has become a rent-capturing plutocracy. The oligarchs are not only Russian, as is too often presumed but rather, and much more so, US, European and Japanese. The decline of democracy is the inevitable product of this concentration of power to the exclusive benefit of the oligopolies.

The new form of capitalist globalisation which corresponds to this transformation – by contrast with the one which characterises the first belle époque – is also important to specify. I have expressed it in a phrase: the passage from plural imperialisms (that of the imperialist powers in permanent conflict with each other) to the collective imperialism of the Triad (the United States, Europe and Japan).

The monopolies that emerged in response to the first crisis of the rates of profit constituted themselves on bases that have reinforced the violence of competition between the major imperialist powers of the time, and led to the armed conflict begun in 1914, which continued through the peace of Versailles and then the Second World War until 1945. That is what Giovanni Arrighi, André Gunder Frank, Immanuel Wallerstein and I described in the 1970s as the 'war of thirty years', a notion that has been taken up by others since then.

By contrast, the second wave of oligopolistic concentration, begun in the 1970s, constituted itself on totally other bases, within the framework of a system which I have described as the collective imperialism of the Triad. In this new imperialist globalisation, the domination of the centres is no longer exercised by the monopoly of industrial production (as had been the case hitherto) but by other means (the control of technologies, financial markets, access to the planet's natural resources, information and communications, weapons of mass destruction). This system, which I have described as 'apartheid on a global scale' implies a permanent war against the states and the peoples of the recalcitrant peripheries, a war already begun in the 1990s by the deployment of military control over the world by the United States and its subordinated NATO allies.

According to my analysis, the financialisation of this system is inextricably linked to its clearly oligopolistic aspect. There is a fundamentally organic relation between them. This point of view is not prevalent, neither in the expansive literature of conventional economists nor in the majority of critical writings on the current crisis.

It is the entire system which henceforth is in difficulty. The facts are clear: the 2008 financial collapse is already producing not a recession but a veritable, profound depression. But beyond this, other dimensions of the crisis of this system had surfaced in public consciousness even before the financial meltdown. We know the sort of labels – energy crisis, food crisis, environmental crisis, climate change – and numerous analyses of these aspects of the contemporary challenges are produced on a daily basis, some of which are of the highest quality.

I remain nonetheless critical about this mode of treating the systemic crisis of capitalism because it excessively isolates the different dimensions of the challenge. I would, therefore, redefine the diverse crises as facets of the same challenge – that of the system of contemporary capitalist globalisation (whether liberal or not), founded upon the principle that the imperialist rent operates on a global scale, to the benefit of the plutocracy of the oligopolies of the imperialist Triad.

The real battle is fought on this decisive ground between the oligopolies – who seek to produce and reproduce the conditions that allow them to appropriate the imperialist rent – and all their victims – the workers of all the countries in the North and the South, the peoples of the dominated peripheries condemned to give up any perspective of development worthy of the name.

Ending the crisis of capitalism or ending capitalism?

This formula – retained in the title of this book – was first suggested by André Gunder Frank and myself in 1974.

The analysis which we developed about the new great crisis that we thought had begun led us to the major conclusion that capital would respond to the challenge with a new wave of concentration on the basis of which it would proceed to massive dislocations. Later developments largely confirmed this. The title of our intervention at a conference organised by *Il Manifesto* in Rome in 1974 ('Let us not wait for 1984', referring to the work by George Orwell) invited the radical left at that time to renounce any strategy of coming to the aid of capital by looking for exits from the crisis in order to seek strategies aimed at an exit from capitalism.

I have pursued this line of analysis with a stubbornness I do not regret. I have suggested a conceptualisation of new forms of domination on the part of the imperialist centres which is grounded in new modes of control that replaced the old monopoly over exclusively industrial production; the rise of the countries referred to as emerging markets has confirmed this conceptualisation. I have described the new globalisation which is being built as an 'apartheid at the global level', calling for the militarised management of the planet and in this way perpetuating in new conditions the polarisation that cannot be dissociated from the expansion of actually existing capitalism.

The second wave of emancipation by the people

There is no alternative to a socialist perspective. The contemporary world is governed by oligarchies: the financial oligarchies in the United States, Europe and Japan who dominate not only economic life but also politics and daily life; Russian oligarchies in their image, which the Russian state tries to control; statocracies in China; autocracies (sometimes hidden behind the appearance of an electoral democracy of low intensity) inscribed into this worldwide system elsewhere across the globe.

The management of contemporary globalisation by these oligarchies is in crisis.

The oligarchies of the North seek to remain in power once the crisis is over. They do not feel threatened. By contrast, the fragility of the power held by the autocracies of the South is clearly visible. The model of globalisation that is currently in place is therefore vulnerable. Will it be questioned by the revolt in the South, as was the case in the previous century? Probably, but that would be cause for sadness. For humanity will only commit itself on the road to socialism – the only humane alternative to chaos – once the powers of the oligarchies, their allies and their servants have been defeated both in the countries of the North and those in the South. Long live the internationalism of the people in the face of the cosmopolitanism of the oligarchies.

Is the reinstatement of the capitalism of financialised and globalised oligopolies possible? Capitalism is liberal by nature, if by liberalism we mean not the pretty label which this notion inspires but the plain and total exercise of the domination of capital not only over work and the economy but over all aspects of social life. There can be no market economy (a vulgar – see Translator's note – expression for capitalism) without a market society. Capital stubbornly pursues this unique objective: money; accumulation for its own sake. Marx, and after him other critical thinkers such as Keynes, understood this perfectly, but not our conventional economists, those on the left included.

This model of total and exclusive domination by capital had been imposed ruthlessly by the ruling classes throughout the previous long crisis up to 1945. Only the triple victory of democracy, socialism and the national liberation of the people allowed a replacement from 1945 to 1980 of this permanent model of the capitalist ideal with the conflictual coexistence of three social, regulated models: the welfare state of Western social democracy, the actually existing socialism in the East and the popular nationalisms in the South. The demise and collapse of these three models made the return of the exclusive domination by capital possible, this time described as the neoliberal phase of capitalism.

I have linked this new liberalism to a series of new characteristics which appears to me to merit the description of senile capitalism. My book with the eponymous title, published in 2001, is probably one of the very few writings at the time which, far from viewing globalised and financialised neoliberalism as the end of history, analysed the system of ageing capitalism as unstable, condemned to eventual collapse, precisely in terms of its financialisation (its 'Achilles' heel', as I wrote then).

Conventional economists have remained persistently deaf to any questioning of their own dogma, so much so that they were unable to foresee the financial collapse of 2008. Those whom the media have portrayed as critical hardly deserve this description. Even Joseph Stiglitz remains convinced that the system as it stands – globalised and financialised liberalism – can be fixed by means of some corrections. Amartya Sen preaches morality without daring to think of actually existing capitalism as it necessarily is.

The social disasters, which the deployment of liberalism – 'the permanent utopia of capital', as I wrote – would cause, have inspired quite a bit of nostalgia in relation to the recent or distant past. But such nostalgia cannot respond to the present challenge. For it is the product of an impoverished critical, theoretical thinking which has gradually stopped itself from understanding the internal contradictions and the limits of the post-1945 systems, whose erosions, diversions and collapses appeared to be unforeseen cataclysms.

However – in the void created by these regressions of critical, theoretical thinking – a consciousness about the new dimensions of the systemic crisis of civilisation managed to chart a path. I am referring here to the ecological movement. But the greens, who have purported to distinguish themselves radically from both the blues (the conservatives and the liberals) and the reds (the socialists) are locked into an impasse since they have failed to link the ecological dimension to the challenge of a radical critique of capitalism.

Everything was therefore ready to ensure the triumph – in fact ephemeral but experienced as definitive – of the alternative described as 'liberal democracy' . This is a miserable kind of thinking – a veritable non-thinking – which ignores Marx's decisive argument about bourgeois democracy's failure to acknowledge that those who decide are not those who are affected by these decisions. Those who decide and benefit from the freedom reinforced by the control over property are nowadays the plutocrats of the capitalism of oligopolies, and states are their debtors. Perforce, the workers and the people affected are little more than their victims. This sort of liberal nonsense might at some point have been credible, at least for a short while, as a result of the diversions of the post-1945 systems. The poverty of the prevailing dogmas could no longer explain the origins of the crisis so that liberal democracy might therefore look like the best of all possible systems.

Today, the powers that be, those who foresaw nothing, are busy restoring the same system. Their possible success, like that of the conservatives in the 1920s – which Keynes had denounced without much of an echo at the time – will only exacerbate the scope of the contradictions which are the root cause of the 2008 financial collapse.

No less serious is the fact that economists on the so-called left have long since embraced the essential tenets of vulgar (see Translator's Note) economics and accepted the erroneous idea that markets are rational. The same economists have focused their efforts on defining the conditions for this market rationality, thereby abandoning Marx, who had discovered the irrationality of markets from the point of view of the workers and the peoples, a perspective deemed obsolete. According to this left-wing perspective capitalism is flexible and adjusts itself to the requirements of progress (technological and even social) if it is constrained in this way. These leftist economists were not prepared to understand that the crisis which has erupted was inevitable. They are even less prepared to confront the challenges that the peoples face as a result. Like the other vulgar economists, they will seek to repair the damage without understanding that it is necessary to pursue another route to be successful – that of overcoming the fundamental logics of capitalism. Instead of looking for exits from capitalism in crisis, they think they can simply exit the crisis of capitalism.

US hegemony in crisis

The G20 summit in London in April 2009 in no way marked the beginning of a reconstruction of the world. And it is perhaps no coincidence amidst the flurry around the G20 that it was followed by a summit meeting of NATO, the right hand of contemporary imperialism, and by the reinforcement of NATO's military involvement in Afghanistan. The permanent war of the North against the South must continue.

We already knew that the governments of the Triad – the United States, Europe and Japan – would pursue the sole goal of restoring the system as it existed before September 2008, and one must not take seriously the interventions at the G20 summit in London by President Obama and Gordon Brown, on the one hand, and those of Sarkozy and Merkel, on the other. Both were aimed at amusing the spectators. The purported differences, identified by the media but without any genuine substance, respond to the exclusive needs of the leaders in question to make the best of themselves in the face of naive public opinion. 'Re-create capitalism', 'moralise financial operations': these and similar grand declarations were made in order to eschew the real questions. That is why restoring the system, which is not impossible, will not solve any problem but will in fact exacerbate the gravity of the crisis. The Stiglitz Commission convened by the United Nations is part of this strategy to trick the public. Obviously, one could not expect otherwise from the oligarchs who control the real power and their political debtors. The point of view I have developed, which puts the emphasis on the inextricable links between the domination of the oligopolies and the necessary financialisation of managing the world economy, is confirmed by the results of the G20 summit.

More interesting is the fact that the invited leaders of the emerging markets chose to remain silent. A single intelligent sentence was said throughout this day of great spectacle – by the Chinese President Hu Jintao, who observed in passing, without insisting and with a (mocking?) smile, that it would be necessary to envisage the creation of a global financial system that is not based on the US dollar. Some commentators immediately linked this – correctly – to Keynes's proposals in 1945.

This remark is a rude reminder that the crisis of the capitalist system of oligopolies is inextricably linked to the crisis of US hegemony, which is on the ropes. But who will replace it? Certainly not Europe, which does not exist apart from or outside Atlanticism and which has no ambition to be independent, as the NATO summit meeting once more confirmed. China? This threat, which the media undoubtedly repeat ad nauseam (a new yellow peril) in order to justify the Atlantic alignment, has no foundation in reality. The Chinese leadership knows that the country does not have such means and they do not have the will. China's strategy is confined to promoting a new globalisation without hegemony – something which neither the United States nor Europe deem acceptable.

The likelihood of a possible evolution in this direction depends once more on the countries of the South. And it is no coincidence that UNCTAD (the United Nations Conference on Trade and Development) is the only institution within the UN umbrella which has taken initiatives that are fundamentally different from those of the Stiglitz Commission. It is no coincidence that UNCTAD's Secretary-General Supachai Panitchpakdi from Thailand, hitherto considered to be a perfect liberal, has dared to propose in a report entitled 'The global economic crisis' of March 2009 realistic ideas that are part of a second wave of a Southern awakening.

For its part, China has begun to build – in a gradual and controlled manner – alternative regional financial systems free from the US dollar. Such initiatives complete on the economic level the promotion of political alliance within the Shanghai Cooperation Organization (SCO), which is a major obstacle to NATO's belligerence.

The NATO summit meeting, convened in the same month as the G20 summit, agreed on Washington's decision not to start a gradual military downsizing but on the contrary to reinforce the scope of its military involvement, always under the misguided pretext of the 'war on terror'. President Obama deployed his talent to save Clinton's and Bush's programme of imposing global military control, which is the only way of prolonging the days of US hegemony now under threat. Obama scored points and obtained a total unconditional surrender from Sarkozy's France – the end of Gaullism – which has now rejoined NATO's military command, something that was difficult during Bush's reign when Washington spoke without intelligence but not without arrogance. Moreover, Obama acted like Bush by ignoring Europe's independence and giving lessons about how Turkey should be allowed to enter the European Union.

Second wave of victorious struggles for the emancipation of workers and peoples

Are new advances in the struggles for the emancipation of the workers and peoples possible?

The political management of the worldwide domination by the capital of oligopolies is necessarily marked by extreme violence. For in order to maintain their status as affluent societies, the countries of the imperialist Triad are henceforth obliged to reserve access to the planet's natural resources for their own exclusive benefit. This new requirement is at the origin of the militarisation of globalisation, which I have elsewhere described as the 'empire of chaos' (the title of a book of mine published in 1992), an expression which others have since taken up.

In line with the Washington project of military control over the planet and the waging of pre-emptive wars under the pretext of the war on terror, NATO has portrayed itself as the representative of the international community and has thereby marginalised the UN – the only institution entitled to speak under this name.

Of course, these real goals cannot be openly acknowledged. In order to mask them, the powers in question have chosen to instrumentalise the discourse on democracy and have arrogated to themselves the right to intervene so as to impose 'respect for human rights'.

At the same time, the absolute power of the new oligarchic plutocracies has hollowed out the substance of the practice of bourgeois democracy. In former times, political negotiation between the different social parties of the hegemonic bloc was necessary for the reproduction of the power of capital. By contrast, the new political management of the society of oligopolistic capitalism, established by means of a systematic depoliticisation, has given rise to a new political culture of 'consensus' (modelled on the example of the United States) which substitutes the consumer and the political spectator for the active citizen – who is a condition for an authentic democracy. This 'liberal virus' (the title of another book of mine, published in 2005) abolishes the opening onto possible alternative choices and replaces it with a consensus that is centred solely on respect for a procedural, electoral democracy.

The demise and collapse of the three social models mentioned above is at the origin of this drama. The page of the first wave of struggles for emancipation has now been turned, that of the second wave has not yet been opened. In the twilight which separates them one can discern the 'monsters', as Gramsci wrote.

In the North, these developments have caused the loss of any real sense of democratic practice. This regression is masked by the pretensions of the so-called post-modern discourse, according to which nations and classes have already left the scene and ceded political space to the individual, who is now the active subject of social transformation.

In the South, other illusions dominate the political realm. The illusion of a capitalist, national and autonomous development that is part of globalisation is powerful among the dominant and the middles classes in emergent markets, fuelled by the immediate success of the last few decades. Nostalgic (para-ethnic or para-religious) illusions about the past are common in the countries excluded from this process.

What is worse, these developments have strengthened the general embrace of the ideology of consumption and the idea that progress is measured by the quantitative growth of consumption. Marx showed that it is the mode of production which determines the mode of consumption and not vice versa, as is claimed by vulgar economics. What is lost sight of in all this is the perspective of a humanist and superior rationality, the basis for the socialist project. The gigantic potential which the application of science and technology offers to the whole of humanity and which would enable the real flourishing of individuals and societies in the North and the South is wasted by the requirements of its subordination to the logics of the unlimited pursuit of the accumulation of capital. What is even worse, the continuous progress of the social productivity of labour is linked to a breathtaking use of the mechanisms of pauperisation (visible at a global scale, for instance in the wholesale attack on peasant societies), as Marx had already understood.

Embracing the ideological alienation which is caused by capitalism does not only adversely affect the affluent societies of the imperialist centres. The peoples of the peripheries, who are for the most part deprived of access to acceptable levels of consumption and blinded by aspirations to consume like the opulent North, are losing consciousness of the fact that the logic of historical capitalism makes the extension of this model to the entire globe impossible.

We can therefore understand the reasons why the 2008 financial collapse was the exclusive result of a sharpening of the internal contradictions peculiar to the accumulation of capital. As a result, only the intervention of forces that embody a positive alternative can offer a way of imagining an exit from the chaos. (In this spirit, I have contrasted the revolutionary way with promoting decadence to overcome the historically obsolete system). And in the current state of affairs, social protest movements, despite their visible growth, remain as a whole unable to question the social order linked to the capitalism of oligopolies in the absence of a coherent political project that can match up to the challenges.

From this point of view, the current situation is markedly different from that which prevailed in the 1930s, when the forces of socialism clashed with fascist parties, producing Nazism, the New Deal and the Popular Fronts.

The deepening of the crisis will not be avoided, even if reinstating the system of domination by the capital of the oligopolies were to be eventually successful, which is not impossible. In this situation, the possible radicalisation of the struggles is not an improbable hypothesis, even if the obstacles remain formidable.

In the countries of the Triad, such a radicalisation would imply that the agenda would be to expropriate the oligopolies, a possibility that seems to be excluded for the foreseeable future. In consequence, the hypothesis that – despite the turmoil caused by the crisis – the stability of the societies of the Triad will not be questioned cannot be discarded. There is a serious risk of a re-run of the 20th century wave of emancipatory struggles, that is to say, a questioning of the system exclusively by some of its peripheries.

A second stage of 'the South's awakening' (*l'éveil du Sud*) – the title of yet another book of mine published in 2007, which offers a reading of the Bandung period as the first stage of this awakening) is now on the agenda. In the best possible scenario, the advances produced in these conditions could force imperialism to retreat, to renounce its demented and criminal project of military control of the world. And if this were the case, then the democratic movement in the countries at the centre of the system could make a positive contribution to the success of this neutralisation strategy. Moreover, the decline of the imperialist rent which benefits the societies at the centre, itself caused by the reorganisation of international equilibria to the advantage of the South (especially China), could help the awakening of a socialist consciousness. However, on the other hand, the societies of the South could still be confronted by the same challenges as in the past, producing the same limits on their progress.

A new internationalism of the workers and the peoples is necessary and possible.

Historical capitalism is all things to everyone, except that it is not durable. It is but a short parenthesis in history. The fundamental questioning of capitalism – which our contemporary thinkers in their overwhelming majority deem neither possible nor desirable – is nonetheless the inescapable condition for the emancipation of the dominated workers and the peoples (those of the peripheries, that is 80 per cent of mankind). And the two dimensions of this challenge are inextricably linked with one another. There will be no exit from capitalism solely by way of the struggle of the people of the North, or solely by the struggle of the dominated people of the South. There will only be an exit from capitalism if and when these two dimensions of the challenge combine with one other. It is far from certain that this will occur, in which case capitalism will be overcome by the destruction of civilisation (beyond the *malaise* in civilisation, to use Freud's terminology) and perhaps of life on the planet. The scenario of a re-run of the 20th century falls short of the requirement for a commitment by mankind to the long route of the transition towards worldwide socialism. The liberal catastrophe requires a renewal of the radical critique of capitalism. The challenge requires the permanent construction/reconstruction of the internationalism of the workers and the peoples in the face of the cosmopolitanism of oligarchic capital.

Constructing this internationalism can only be envisaged by successful, new, revolutionary advances (like those begun in Latin America and Nepal) which offer the perspective of an overcoming of capitalism.

In the countries of the South, the battle of the states and the nations for a negotiated globalisation without hegemonies – the contemporary form of delinking – supported by the organisation of the demands of the popular classes can circumscribe and limit the powers of the oligopolies of the imperialist Triad. The democratic forces in the countries of the North must support this battle. Real engagement with the challenge is eschewed by the proposed democratic discourse. This has been accepted as it stands, together with the humanitarian interventions in its name, by a majority of the left, just like the miserable practice of giving aid.

In the countries of the North, the oligopolies are already clearly forms of the common good whose management cannot be left to sectional private interests alone (the crisis has highlighted the catastrophic results of such an approach). An authentic left must dare to envision nationalisation as the first inescapable stage of the socialisation of the oligopolies by deepening democratic practice. The current crisis makes it possible to conceive a common front of social and political forces, bringing together all the victims of the exclusive power of the ruling oligarchies.

The first wave of struggles for socialism, that of the 20th century, showed the limits of European social democracies, of the communisms of the Third International and of the popular nationalism of the Bandung era, which brought the demise and collapse of their socialist ambitions. The second wave, that of the 21st century, must draw lessons from this. In particular, one lesson is to associate the socialisation of economic management and the deepening of the democratisation of society. There will be no socialism without democracy, but equally no democratic advance outside a socialist perspective.

These strategic goals invite us to think about the construction of convergences in diversity (referring here to the formula used by the World Forum of Alternatives) of forms of organisation and the struggles of the dominated and exploited classes. It is not my intention to condemn from the outset the convergences of these forms, which in their own way would retrieve the traditions of social democracy, communism and popular nationalism, or would diverge from them.

According to this perspective, it seems to me to be necessary to think the renewal of a creative Marxism. Marx has never been so useful and necessary in order to understand and transform the world, today even more so than yesterday. Being Marxist in this spirit is to begin with Marx and not to stop with him, or Lenin or Mao, as conceived and practised by the historical Marxists of the previous century. It is to render unto Marx that which is owed to him: the intelligence to have begun a modern critical thinking, a critique of capitalist reality and a critique of its political, ideological and cultural representations (see Translator's note). A creative Marxism must pursue the goal of enriching this critical thinking par excellence. It must not fear to integrate all the input of reflection, in all areas, including those which have wrongly been considered to be foreign by the dogmas of historical Marxisms of the past.

The structure of this book

This book is composed of the arguments sustaining the theses that have been briefly presented in this Introduction.

Chapter 1 opens with a reminder, not of the unfolding financial

INTRODUCTION

crisis (excellent presentations of which can be found elsewhere), but of the origin of the causes that made them fatal (foreseeable and correctly predicted by a few). I have situated these causes in the development of the capitalism of generalised oligopolies and collective imperialism, and not in the expansion of credit, which is a consequence and not a cause.

There follow two chapters dedicated to a reading of capitalism over a long period. Chapter 2 discusses the diversity of the responses to the growing contradictions of the old systems which here and there opened up the way to it (comparing Europe, the Mediterranean and the Middle East with the Chinese world). Then, in Chapter 3, there is a presentation of historical (Atlantic) capitalism, which was to become the definitive form of this response, based on its principal characteristic: accumulation through dispossession. The contrast between the centres and the peripheries generated by this permanent form of accumulation in historical capitalism governs, in its turn, the dominant contradiction that accompanies capitalism as it develops and, based on this, the struggles in which its victims are engaged. The fight of the peoples of the periphery is accorded its full place: it shaped the first wave of struggles (in the 20th century) and will probably, for the same reasons, shape the second wave, yet to come (in the 21st century).

It is more than ever necessary, at the dawn of a possible opening to this second wave of struggles, to recall, however briefly, the advances and retreats experienced by the struggles for emancipation by the workers and peoples in the 20th century. I do this in Chapter 4.

It is not by chance that I have placed the new agrarian question, which is the subject of Chapter 5, at the heart of the challenge for the 21st century. I had no difficulty in making this choice among other possibilities. My thesis is that the development of the struggles in this field, the responses that will be given through them in the future by the peasant societies of the South (almost half of humanity) will largely condition the capacity (or not) of the workers and peoples to make progress on the route to socialism.

This is the challenge that confronts the construction/reconstruction of the internationalism of the workers and peoples in the face of the cosmopolitanism of oligarchic capital. In Chapter 6 I try to show how and why the humanist discourse that is proposed and accepted by most of the left, such as it is, is not up to meeting this challenge.

The last chapter, Chapter 7, concerns Marx and Marxism, communism and internationalism. Never before has Marx been so useful and necessary to understanding and changing the world situation as he is today.

Note

1. 'Monopoly rent' was defined by Marx as the difference between the price of production and market price where market price is set not by the average profit that results from equalisation of the rate of profits over time; instead the price is set by a few cartels or corporations. In the current imperialist epoch, a small number of oligopolies sets the world prices in various sectors of production (e.g. oil, medicines, biotechnology, agricultural inputs), and thus monopoly rent is often referred to as imperialist rent or rent of oligopolies. Where finance capital exercises the same control over prices, the term financialised monopoly rent is sometimes used.

References

Amin, Samir (1992) *The Empire of Chaos*, New York, NY, Monthly Review Press
Amin, Samir (2002) *Beyond Senile Capitalism*, Paris, Presses Universitaires de France (PUF)
Amin, Samir (2005) *The Liberal Virus: Permanent War and the Americanization of the World*, New York, NY, Monthly Review Press
Amin, Samir (2007) *L'Éveil du Sud*, Paris, le Temps des Cerises

The financial collapse of liberal globalisation

The financial collapse of September 2008 was foreseeable and predicted by those rare analysts who had not succumbed to the discourse of conventional economics, liberal and others (of the 'left'). This collapse certainly initiated a new period of depression and chaos. And the shape of the system that will emerge is difficult to define precisely with any degree of plausibility. Everything is possible, for better or for worse. It is an open question. Through their successes or failures, political and social struggles will shape the future, which is more uncertain than ever.

However, the financial collapse is not only the beginning of the transformations to come. It is also the end of the evolution of the system and of its changes. It is the end, not only of some 20 years of the financial explosion, which is blindingly obvious today, but, beyond that, the end of the long crisis that began in 1968–1971.

I insist on this last point precisely because it is absent in the analyses of the 'financial crisis' (at least of those that I know) and even of the 'systemic crisis' that is associated with it – in the better cases.

After the Second World War, globalised capitalism experienced a period of marked growth which lasted for a quarter of a century, from 1945 to 1970.

The reasons for this growth are obvious. The power relationships were more favourable to the working classes (the victory of democracy over fascism); to socialism (the victory of the Red Army over the Nazis); and to the peoples of Asia and Africa (who set out to reconquer their independence). This created the conditions for the 'glorious' decades (the catching-up of Europe and Japan vis-à-vis the United States, the only beneficiary of the war) and for those years of the 'development' of the South.

At the same time, this growth facilitated the adjustment of capital to the requirements of the workers and of peoples. Growth, which was strong, offered capital opportunities for the investment it required to feed itself. The 'moderate' rate of returns (in relative historical terms) on capital was compensated by solid and continued growth in the volume of profits. This moderate rate represented one side of the reality of this period, the others being the growth in real wages (growing parallel with average social productivity) and the acceptance by the imperial powers of concessions to the countries of the periphery that had regained their independence.

The viability of the system was supported, on the international political level, by military bipolarity (United States/Soviet Union) and peaceful coexistence (at the time people even spoke of the convergence of the eastern and western systems, which Jan Tinbergen predicted would increase).

The system was legitimised by a series of powerful ideological discourses that complemented each other: the social-democratic/ Keynesian discourse in the West; that of actually existing socialism (see Translator's note) in the East; and that of development in the South. They all shared the same vision of 'peace and social progress'. At the heart of the system in the developed countries, it was felt that the management of capital should be entrusted to capitalist technocrats rather than to the formal owners of capital (the shareholders). John Kenneth Galbraith expressed this optimistic vision of a capitalism that had finally become socially responsible, whose leaders were more interested in innovation and in extending their enterprises than in the rate of their remuneration (which was, even so, a comfortable one) and in the useless distribution of profits to shareholders (Keynes predicted their euthanasia). This system has given what it has given, but it gradually ran out of steam for reasons that I have analysed elsewhere, so I shall not repeat them here.

This capitalist system entered into crisis from 1968 (a political crisis and erosion of the legitimacy of its discourse) and 1971 (the abandoning of the convertibility of the dollar to gold).

The present crisis is nothing more than one stage (which is certainly new) in this long, drawn-out crisis dating back to the

1 THE FINANCIAL COLLAPSE OF LIBERAL GLOBALISATION

1970s. It has been marked by a weakening in the rates of growth and of investment, which have never recovered – and I insist on the *'never'* – the levels that they attained in the post-1945 period. Triumphant liberalism from the 1990s onwards has changed nothing in that respect.

Only a few of us, in the 1970s, spoke of the structural crisis (which is described as systemic these days). How was dominant capital going to meet the challenge?

At that time André Gunder Frank and I had imagined that the logic of capital would opt for a '1984' (it was in 1974), based on a massive delocalisation of ordinary industrial production activities towards the countries of the periphery and the recentralisation of activities in the centres around the monopolies that guaranteed them the control of the delocalised production and enabled them to levy rent on it. I will not dwell here on the developments that I proposed concerning these new 'monopolies' of the imperialist centres (control of technologies, access to natural resources, global finance). Delocalisation above all made it possible, we said at the time, to break the relationship between wages and productivity and to reduce real wages (or their growth), which were at the centre of the whole system.

I do not believe that what has happened since has invalidated our precocious theses which were scornfully dismissed as rants by our 'left-wing' economists (not to speak of the liberals). With the exception of the Italian *Manifesto*, they were hardly given serious attention in Europe or in the United States, so far as I know, alas except perhaps by Margaret Thatcher and Ronald Reagan and a few senior officials in countries of the South (I was invited to come and speak about our theses ... in China!). Because in fact, from 1980, Thatcher and Reagan decided to do what we had feared they would do.

This strategy of capital was set in motion in 1981 (at the G7 meeting at Cancún) and it accelerated during the 1990s after the collapse of the Soviet Union. It took on the name of 'neoliberalism': privatisation and liberalisation aimed at opening up new frontiers for the expansion of capital; the globalised opening that would enable delocalisation; the imposition of structural adjustment programmes on the countries of the South; and the liberalisation of the rates of interest and currency exchange.

It is important to understand the transformations of the capital system itself that conditioned the success of this operation and even imposed it. There were two transformations at the origin of this so-called 'neoliberal' option: the emergence of a generalised capitalism of oligopolies (I insist on the adjective 'generalised' as oligopolies are no novelty in the history of capitalism) and the emergence of the collective imperialism of the Triad (the United States, Europe and Japan). I will return to these later, but I emphasise their decisive role, because most of the analyses of the 'systemic crisis' do not. I believe, moreover, that if you neglect to spell out all the developments from 1990 as they impact on these transformations, you inevitably view the vertiginous expansion of credit that led to the 2008 crisis as the result of a 'deviation', as being without any cause. Or else the cause originated in a 'theoretical blunder' (neoliberalism). But this deviation was a necessary and perfectly logical consequence from the viewpoint of the management of the world by the oligopolies. The essential relationship between oligopoly rent and financialisation will be dealt with in subsequent pages.

Understanding how all the dimensions of what is today called the 'systemic crisis' revolve around these two decisive transformations is the only way of situating them (the energy crisis, the food crisis and others) in a framework that assigns them their true place. Only thus is it possible to identify, beyond the general nature of these challenges (the option in favour of high-level energy consumption which has such disastrous consequences, for example), the issues and the different counterstrategies that are possible and effective for the workers and for the peoples. If all this is not understood, the risk is that people will be satisfied with pious wishes or, worse still, adjust to minor changes in the same system (under so-called 'ecological' management). Capital will then continue to keep the initiative.

The neoliberal option (1990–2008) has not extricated capitalism from its long crisis (which started in 1971). It imprisoned capitalism still further, as can be seen from the weakness in growth and in investments to expand and deepen the productive systems.

Weakness of growth? How then to explain the accelerating growth in the emerging countries? It is important to realise that this is not 'the exception that proves the rule' but an essential

1 THE FINANCIAL COLLAPSE OF LIBERAL GLOBALISATION

part of the rule, as this acceleration is linked to the sought-after delocalisations. That this emergence can create problems in the longer term is beyond dispute. But that constitutes another series of questions, problems and concerns.

The real objective of the liberal option has not been to reinstall growth – even if the liberal discourse claims that it is. The real objective was to proceed to a redistribution of income in favour of capital, and of the income appropriated by capital in favour of the rent of oligopolies. These two objectives have been fulfilled to a far greater extent than the 'left' could have imagined. The success of this option has indeed weakened growth; it has not happened 'in spite' of it.

And, in turn, this success – and the weakening of growth that it requires – has imposed all the deviations of finance capital.

On the basis of this analysis it seemed to me evident that the neoliberal option would not be viable. I said in 2002 that I had 'no crystal ball' but predicted that the collapse would occur within 10 years.

The financial collapse of September 2008 thus initiated a worsening of the systemic crisis of capitalism. To understand the nature of this crisis and what is at stake, and on that basis to imagine the possible forms of the different alternative systems that will gradually emerge from the responses that will be made by the dominant powers, the states and the governing classes, as well as the workers and the dominated peoples, it is necessary to move beyond analysing the unwinding of the financial crisis, in its narrowest sense. But it is not enough, either, to juxtapose this last analysis and that of other crises, in particular: (1) the crisis of accumulation in the real, productive economy; (2) the energy crisis, concerning (a) the dwindling of fossil fuel resources, (b) the consequences of the growth caused by the model using this energy (possible effects on the climate included), and (c) the consequences of substitution policies (agrofuels); and (3) the crisis of peasant societies subjected to accelerated destruction and the food crisis that is linked to it. It is necessary to include all the dimensions of this major systemic crisis in an integrated analysis.

So I shall return to the major transformations that have developed over the last decades. Although they started to evolve a long time ago, I believe that the quantitative change has become a qualitative leap forward.

The first of these transformations concerns the degree of the centralisation of capital in its dominant sectors. This is immeasurably greater than it was only some 40 years ago. True, monopolies and oligopolies were not new in the history of capitalism, from the mercantilist era until the emergence of trusts and cartels at the end of the 19th century (analysed by Hilferding, Hobson and Lenin). But today we should call it a generalised capitalism of oligopolies that now dominates all the fields of economic life.

I deduce two major consequences from this observation. First, that this transformation has given a new face to imperialism. In the past this term was always used in the plural, which was apparent from the permanent conflicts between the imperialist powers. Now we should refer to the collective imperialism of the Triad in the singular.

The second major, qualitative transformation concerns the natural resources of the planet. These are no longer so abundant for unlimited access to their exploitation to be considered possible. They have become relatively much rarer (if not in the process of being exhausted) and for this reason their access cannot be open to all.

The list of 'what is new' in the organisation of modern societies is much greater than the fields considered here. Many books emphasise, for example, the scientific and technological revolution of our time (information technology, space, nuclear energy, deep-sea exploitation, the production of new materials, etc). This is all very important and beyond dispute. Nevertheless, I refuse to approach this dimension of reality through the 'technologist' discourses that dominate the subject, considering these innovations as the main driver of history and therefore calling on society to 'adjust' to the constraints that they impose. On the contrary, in the analyses that I am proposing, technologies are themselves shaped by the dominant social relationships. In the field of international relations, the possibility of 'new powers' emerging cannot be excluded. In the field of social relationships the list of 'new developments' could indeed appear to be unlimited, for example, with the labour market and the organisation of productive systems, or the erosion of old forms of political expression in favour of new

1 THE FINANCIAL COLLAPSE OF LIBERAL GLOBALISATION

affirmations – or renewed or reinforced – of gender, ethnic, religious and cultural identities. However, I think it is necessary to link the analysis of these realities to the logic of the reproduction of the system, characterised by those of the major transformations that I have spelt out.

The crisis is systemic in that the continuation of the model deployed by capitalism over the last decades has become impossible. The page will necessarily be turned in a 'transition' period (of crisis), for a shorter or longer time, orderly or chaotic. 'Another world is possible' proclaimed the 'alternative world movement' at Porto Alegre, Brazil. I say, 'Another world is in the process of emerging', which could be still more barbaric than the present, but which could also be better, to varying degrees.

The dominant social forces will try, in the conflicts that are destined to become more acute, to maintain their privileged positions. But they will not be able to do so unless they break with many of the principles and practices that until now have been associated with their domination, particularly renouncing democracy, international law and respect for the rights of the peoples of the South. If they succeed in doing so, tomorrow's world will be based on what I have called 'apartheid at the world level'. Will it be a new phase of capitalism or a system that is qualitatively new and different? It is worthwhile discussing this question.

The workers and the peoples who will be the victims of this barbaric evolution could put to flight the reactionary social and political forces (which are not 'liberal' as they like to describe themselves) that are at work. They are capable of taking the full measure of the issues of this systemic crisis, of freeing themselves from the illusive responses that seem to prevail at the present moment, to invent appropriate forms of organisation and action and to transcend the fragmentation of their struggles and overcome the contradictions that result from it. Will they have then 'invented' or 'reinvented' the socialism of the 21st century? Or will they have only advanced in that direction, along the long route of the secular transition of capitalism to socialism? I think it is more likely to be the latter.

Globalisation – a phenomenon that is inherent to capitalism as it deepens during the successive phases of its expansion – means that the world of tomorrow will not be better unless the peoples of the South (who represent 80 per cent of humanity), struggle to make themselves felt. If this does not happen the world cannot be better. There are no grounds for believing that, in a movement of humanist generosity, the workers of the North – themselves as much victims of the existing system – could shape a better world system for the peoples of the South.

The domination of the oligopolies is the basis of a financialisation in disarray.

The phenomenon of contemporary capitalism described as financialisation consists of the expansion of investments on the monetary and financial markets. This exponential expansion, unprecedented in history, started a quarter of a century ago and has increased the volume of operations conducted annually on these markets to more than $2,000,000 billion, as opposed to about $50,000 billion for the world's GDP (gross domestic product) and $15,000 billion for international trade.

This financialisation has been made possible both by the generalisation of the flexible exchange system (the rates of which are determined each day by what is called 'the market') and by the parallel deregulation of the rates of interest (also abandoned to supply and demand). In these conditions, operations on the monetary and financial markets no longer constitute the counterpart of trade in goods and services, but are now stimulated almost exclusively by the concern of economic agents to protect themselves from fluctuations in the rates of exchange and interest.

Clearly, the astronomical expansion of these operations to cover themselves from risk in no way corresponds to the immediate expectations of those who are mobilising the means. Elementary common sense dictates that the more the means are multiplied for reducing the risks for a certain operation, the greater the collective risk becomes. But the conventional economists are not equipped to understand this. They need to believe in the absurd dogma of the self-regulation of the markets, without which the entire construction of the so-called 'market economy' would collapse. The market economy, which I have described elsewhere as the theory of an imaginary system that has no relationship to real capitalism, is the cornerstone of the ideology (in the vulgar – see Translator's

1 THE FINANCIAL COLLAPSE OF LIBERAL GLOBALISATION

note – and negative sense of the term) of capitalism, its way of giving it an appearance of legitimacy.

It is therefore not surprising that conventional economists, in spite of their arrogance, have been incapable of foreseeing what, for others, was evident. And when the collapse actually happened, they could find no other excuse other than it was purely 'accidental', mistakes in calculations concerning 'sub-primes' and others. For them it could only be caused by minor accidents, without dramatic consequences, which could be quickly corrected.

The expansion of the monetary and financial markets, which inevitably led to catastrophe, was extremely well analysed, even before the collapse of September 2008, by critical political economists, particularly by François Morin, Frédéric Lordon, Elmar Altvater, Peter Gowan, me and some others (alas, all too few). There is nothing here to add to these analyses of how these events developed.

But it is necessary to go further, for limiting the financial crisis to a financial analysis implies that the only causes were those directly responsible for it. In other words, it was the dogma of the liberalisation of the monetary and financial markets and their 'deregulation' that was at the origin of the disaster. But that is only true at a first, immediate, reading of the reality. Beyond that the question concerns the identification of the social interests that are behind this adherence to dogmas concerning the deregulation of these markets.

Here again, the banks and other financial institutions (insurance companies, pension and hedge funds) seem to have been the main beneficiaries of this expansion, which makes it possible for the official discourses to make them exclusively responsible for the disaster. But, in fact, financialisation benefited the oligopolies as a whole, 40 per cent of their profits deriving from their financial operations alone. And these oligopolies control both the dominant sectors of the real productive economy and the financial institutions.

Why, therefore, have the oligopolies deliberately chosen the financialisation path for the system as a whole? The reason is quite simply that it enables them to take for themselves a growing proportion of all the profits from the real economy. The apparently insignificant rates of gain on each financial operation produces, taking into account the gigantic scale of these operations, considerable profits. These are the result of a redistribution of the mass of surplus value generated in the real economy and they constitute the rents of the monopolies. It is easy to understand, therefore, that the high rate of yields of financial investments (around 15 per cent) has, as a corollary, mediocre rates of yields for investments in the productive economy (around 5 per cent). This levy on the global mass of profits operated by the financial rent of the oligopolies makes it impossible not to associate the cause (the oligopolistic character of contemporary capitalism) with its consequence (financialisation, that is, a preference for financial investment compared with investment in the real economy).

The monetary and financial market thus has a dominant position in the market system. It is the market where the oligopolies (and not only the banks) deduct their monopoly rent on the one hand and, on the other, compete among themselves for the sharing of this rent. Conventional economists ignore this hierarchy in the markets, replacing it with an abstract discourse on the 'economy of generalised markets'.

The expansion of the monetary and financial market thus inhibits investment in the real economy, limiting growth. In turn, this weakening in the general growth of the economy affects jobs, with its well-known consequences (unemployment, a growing precariousness and the stagnation – if not reduction – of real wages, which are disconnected from progress in productivity). The monetary and financial markets in turn dominate the world of work. All these mechanisms together force the submission of the economy as a whole (the 'markets') to the dominant monetary and financial market, producing an ever-increasing inequality in income distribution (that no one denies). The market for productive investment (and hence for work) suffers both from the reduction of its apparent direct profitability (the price of the levy for oligopoly rent) and also from reduced final demand (weakened by the inequality in sharing the income).

The domination of the financialised oligopolies boxes up the economy in a crisis of capital accumulation, which is both a crisis in demand ('under-consumption') and a crisis in profitability.

1 THE FINANCIAL COLLAPSE OF LIBERAL GLOBALISATION

We should now be able to understand why the dominant powers (governments of the Triad), themselves at the services of the oligopolies, have no other project than to re-establish this same financialised system, for the oligopolies need to expand financially in order to maintain their domination over the economy and society. Questioning the domination of the monetary and financial market over markets as a whole is to question the monopoly rent of the oligopolies.

Can the policies being followed for this purpose be effective? I believe that it is not impossible to restore the system as it was before the crisis of the autumn of 2008. But two conditions need to be met.

The first is that the state and the central banks have to inject into the system the huge quantities of finance that erase all of the rotten debts and restore credibility and profitability to the re-establishment of financial expansion. The sums required are indeed astronomical, as some (myself included) foresaw several years before the debacle of the autumn of 2008, against the opinion of conventional economists and the 'IMF experts' (International Monetary Fund), who did not join us in our estimations until three months after the disaster. But now it is possible to believe that the powers that be will bring this injection up to the level required.

As for the second, the consequences of this injection have to be accepted by society, for the workers in general, and the peoples of the South in particular, are necessarily the victims. These policies are not aimed at re-launching the real economy through re-launching wage demand (as Keynesianism proposed in former times) but, on the contrary, maintaining the levy composed of the rent of the oligopolies, and this, necessarily, would be to the detriment of the real wages of the workers. Those in power callously envisage the aggravation of the crisis of the real economy, unemployment, precariousness and the deterioration of pensions insured by the pension funds. The workers are already reacting and will probably react more in the coming months and years. But their struggles remain fragmented and with no prospects because of the way they are at present being waged; these protests are 'controllable' by the power of the oligopolies and the states at their service.

There is a big difference between the political and social conjuncture of our epoch and that of the 1930s. At that time, two camps of social forces confronted each other: the left, which called for socialism, composed of communists (the Soviet Union gave the impression of success at that time) and of authentic social democrats, and the right, which could get support from powerful fascist movements. This is why, in response to the 1930 crisis, in some places there were developments like the New Deal and popular fronts, while in others Nazism. The current political conjuncture is radically different. The failure of Sovietism and the rallying of socialists to social liberalism has drastically weakened the political vision of workers, who are deprived of prospects and the capacity to express an authentic alternative socialism.

The current crisis of oligopoly capitalism was not the result of a rise in social struggles forcing the retreat of the oligopolies' ambitions. It is the exclusive result of the internal contradictions peculiar to its accumulation system. In my opinion, the distinction is absolutely central between the crisis of a system produced by the explosion of its internal contradictions and that of a society that suffers the assault of progressive social forces aiming at transforming the system. On this difference will depend the different possible outcomes. In a situation of the first type, chaos becomes a major probability and it is only in a situation of the second type that a progressive outcome is possible. The main political question today is thus to know whether the social victims of the existing system will become capable of constituting an independent, radical, consistent and positive alternative.

If not, the restoration of the financialised rent oligopolies to power is not impossible. But, in this case, the system will only withdraw to get a better run-in and a new financial debacle, still more serious, will be inevitable, because the 'adjustments' envisaged for managing the financial markets are far from sufficient as long as the power of the oligopolies is not questioned.

It remains to be seen how the states and the peoples of the South are going to respond to the challenge. Here we should analyse this challenge which has been exacerbated by globalised financialisation.

It is absolutely indispensable to take into account the question of natural resources and the North–South conflict. No effective strategy in response to the challenge can ignore these issues.

1 THE FINANCIAL COLLAPSE OF LIBERAL GLOBALISATION

There are key questions concerning both the use that an economic and social system makes of the natural resources of the planet and the philosophical conception of the relationships between human beings (and within society) on the one hand, and between humans and nature on the other. The response to these questions that a society has given in the past describes the rationality that governs its economic and social management.

Historically, capitalism has mainly ignored these considerations. It established a strictly economic rationality with a short-term vision ('the depreciation of the future') and was based on the principle that natural resources are generally put at the free disposal of society and, what is more, in unlimited quantities. The only exception is when certain resources are privately appropriated, as the land or mining resources, but subordinating their utilisation to the exclusive requirements of the profitability for capital, which exploits the potential. The rationality of this system is therefore narrow and becomes socially irrational as soon as these resources become scarce, even exhausted, or when their usage, in the forms imposed by the economic profitability of capitalism, produces dangerous long-term consequences (destruction of biodiversity, climate change).

I propose here not to discuss these fundamental aspects of the question of society and nature's relationship, still less to intervene in the philosophical debates about the development of the different ways of thinking about the problem. My proposal is much more modest and concerns only access to the use of the planet's resources and their distribution, in theory and in practice, whether it is equal and open to all peoples or, on the contrary, reserved for the exclusive benefit of some.

From that viewpoint, our modern world system has now undergone a qualitative transformation of decisive significance. Some major natural resources have become considerably rarer – in relative terms – than they were even 50 years ago, and their drying-up constitutes a threat that is perhaps real (this can certainly be debated). There is now an awareness that their access cannot be open to all any longer. This, independent of how they are used, endangers the future of the planet, according to some (although not everyone). The countries of the North (and I deliberately use this vague term not to specify either the states or the peoples) intend to have exclusive access to these resources for their own use, whether these resources would be used as at present – that is, based on waste and endangering a future that is not far off – or whether they would be subject to considerable corrective regulations, as certain greens propose.

The egoism of the countries of the North was brutally expressed by former US president George W. Bush when he declared: 'The American way of life is not negotiable' (a phrase that his successors, whoever they may be, will not discuss). Many in Europe and Japan feel the same way, even if they refrain from declaring it. This egoism simply means that access to these scarce natural resources will largely be denied to the countries of the South (80 per cent of humanity), whether the latter intend to use these resources in a similar way to that of the North, which is wasteful and dangerous, or whether they envisage more economical forms.

It goes without saying that this prospect is unacceptable to the countries of the South, in theory and in practice. Besides, the markets are not necessarily able to meet the requirements that guarantee the exclusive access of the rich countries to these resources. Certain countries of the South can mobilise large sums in order to make themselves recognised on these markets for access to resources. At the last resort, the only guarantee for the countries of the North lies in their military superiority.

The militarisation of globalisation is the expression of this egoistic attitude. It is not the result of a passing aberration of the Washington administration. The plan for the military control of the planet by the US armed forces was established by former president Bill Clinton, pursued by Bush and will be continued by current President Barack Obama. Of course, to attain these objectives Washington always intends to use this 'advantage' for its own benefit, in particular to compensate for its own financial deficiencies and maintain its leadership, if not hegemonic position, within the camp of the North. The subordinate allies of the Triad are very much aligned along the Washington plan to militarily control the planet. Neither the Atlanticism of the Europeans nor the submission of Tokyo to the views of Washington concerning Asia and the Pacific seem likely to disintegrate, at least for the moment. Of course the 'missions' – preventive wars, the fight against 'terrorism' – in which the US armed forces and their subordinate allies

1 THE FINANCIAL COLLAPSE OF LIBERAL GLOBALISATION

of NATO (North Atlantic Treaty Organisation) are engaged will always be presented in discourses about a 'defence of democracy' (if not its exportation), of the 'defence of the rights of peoples to self-determination' (at least for some, but not for others). But these packages only deceive those who want to be deceived. For the peoples of the South they are just reminded of the permanence of the old colonial tradition of the 'civilising mission'. The real exclusive objective of the North's military programme is the control of the world's resources. This was plain when Washington recently decided to complete its system of military 'Regional Commands' and bases by creating an 'African Command'. The United States, and behind it Europe, thus aims at controlling oil (in the Gulf of Guinea, Sudan), uranium (Niger, Sudan), rare metals (Congo, southern Africa), and nothing more.

The North/South conflict has become the centre of the major contradictions of contemporary capitalist/imperialist globalisation. And it is in this sense that the conflict cannot be separated from the one that opposes the domination of oligopolistic capitalism against the progressive and socialist ambitions that could put forward alternatives, here and there, in the South and in the North. 'Another, better world' is not possible if the interests of the peoples who constitute 80 per cent of humanity are regarded with almost total contempt in the dominant opinion of the rich countries. Humanitarianism is not an acceptable substitute to international solidarity in struggle.

The countries in the centre of the world capitalist system have always benefited from what I have described as 'imperialist rent' and the capital accumulation in these centres has always involved 'accumulation through dispossession' of the peoples of the periphery. Today's claim to reserve access to the world's main resources for the rich alone constitutes its new, contemporary form.

What then are the conditions for a positive response to the challenge? It is not enough to say that the interventions of states can modify the rules of the game and attenuate the aberrations. It is also necessary to define the logic and the social impact. Of course, one might imagine a return to the formula of public/private partnerships or a mixed economy, as during the 30 'glorious years' in Europe and the Bandung era in Asia and Africa when state capitalism was largely dominant and there were serious social policies. But this kind of intervention by the state is no longer on the agenda. And are the progressive social forces strong enough to impose such a transformation? In my humble opinion, they are not.

The real alternative involves overturning the exclusive power of the oligopolies, which is inconceivable without finally nationalising them for a management that is in line with a progressive democratic socialisation. The end of capitalism? I don't think so. I think, on the other hand, that new patterns in social power relationships can force capital to make adjustments in response to the claims of the popular classes (see Translator's note) and peoples, this on the condition that the social struggles – still fragmented and on the whole defensive – succeed in drawing up a coherent political alternative. If so, the beginning of the long transition from capitalism to socialism becomes possible. Progress in that direction is obviously unequal from one country to another and from one phase of implementation to another.

There are many dimensions of a possible, desirable alternative and they concern all aspects of economic, social and political life. In the countries of the North the challenge means that the general opinion must not be allowed to limit itself to the defence of their privileges vis-à-vis the peoples of the South. The necessary internationalism must take the form of anti-imperialism, not humanitarianism.

In the countries of the South, the crisis provides an opportunity to renew a national, popular and democratically self-managed development, subordinating its relationships with the North to its own needs, in other words, delinking. This involves national control over the monetary and financial markets; recovering the usage of natural resources; overturning globalised management dominated by the oligopolies (the World Trade Organisation – WTO) and the military control of the planet by the United States and its associates; and freeing themselves from both the illusions of a national, autonomous capitalism and a backward-looking system with its own enduring myths.

The agrarian question is more than ever at the core of the options to be taken in the countries of the Third World. A development worthy of the name cannot be based on growth – even

1 THE FINANCIAL COLLAPSE OF LIBERAL GLOBALISATION

strong growth – that exclusively benefits a minority, even if it is 20 per cent of the population, leaving most of the population abandoned to stagnation, if not pauperisation. This model of development, associated with exclusion, is the only one that capitalism can offer the countries of the periphery in its global system. Political democracy (which is evidently the exception in these conditions), when it is associated with social regression, remains fragile indeed. But a national and popular alternative that associates the democratisation of society with social progress, that is, with a perspective of development that integrates – and does not exclude – the popular classes, requires a political strategy of rural development based on the guarantee of access to land for all peasants.

Moreover, the policies recommended by the dominant powers – accelerating the privatisation of agricultural land, treated as a commodity – are provoking the massive rural exodus that we are witnessing today. Modern industrial development cannot absorb this over-abundant labour force, which is piling up in urban slums. There is a direct link between suppressing the guarantee of access to land for the peasants and accentuating migratory pressures.

Does regional integration that promotes the emergence of new centres of development constitute a form of resistance and an alternative? There is no simple reply to this question. The dominant oligopolies are not hostile to regional integrations that are in line with the logic of capitalist/imperialist globalisation. The European Union (EU) and the regional common markets of Latin America, Asia and Africa are examples of forms of regionalisation that become obstacles to the emergence of progressive and socialist alternatives. Can another form of regionalisation be conceived that is capable of supporting the option of national and popular development and opening the way towards the long, secular transition to socialism for the peoples and nations of the planet? While this question is not relevant for the giants like China and India, it cannot be dismissed from debates concerning Latin America, the Arab world, Africa, South East Asia and even Europe. As far as this last region is concerned, is it not possible to envisage the destruction of the EU institutions, the purpose of which was to confine the peoples of this continent in so-called liberal (i.e. reactionary) capitalism and an Atlantic alignment? This could be the precondition for its eventual reconstruction (if it were to be considered useful) with a socialist perspective. For the countries of the South as a whole, is it possible to envisage a new political Bandung that would reinforce the capacity of the countries of the three continents to compel the collective imperialism of the Triad to back down? What would the conditions be?

There would need to be progress in both the North and South in the internationalism of workers and peoples, who are the sole guarantee for the reconstruction of a better, multipolar and democratic world and the only alternative to the barbarism of an ageing capitalism. If capitalism has got to the point that it considers half of humanity a 'superfluous population', might it not be that capitalism itself has now become a mode of social organisation that is superfluous?

There is no feasible alternative that does not have a socialist perspective.

Quite apart from necessary agreements on the strategy of stages, based on the construction of the converging of struggles, respecting diversity and the progress that these struggles can contribute to the long route to world socialism, it is essential to reflect and debate on the socialist/communist objective: imagining emancipation from market and other alienations, imagining the democratisation of social life in all its dimensions and imagining modes of managing production, from the local to the world level, that correspond to the needs of a genuine democracy associated with social progress.

Evidently, if the capitalist/imperialist world system as it actually exists is based on the growing exclusion of the peoples who constitute the majority of humanity, and if the manner of using natural resources resulting from the logic of capitalist profitability is both wasteful and dangerous, the socialist/communist alternative cannot ignore the challenges posed by these realities. There has to be another 'style of consumption and living' than that which apparently gives happiness to the peoples of the rich countries and which exists in the imagination of its victims. The expression of a 'solar socialism', proposed by Elmar Altvater, must be taken seriously. Socialism cannot be capitalism, corrected by equal access to its benefits at the national and world levels. It must be qualitatively superior or it will not happen.

References

Altvater, Elmar (2008) 'The plagues of capitalism: energy crisis, climate collapse, hunger and financial instabilities', paper presented at the Forum Mondial des Alternatives (FMA), Caracas, Venezuela

Amin, Samir et al (forthcoming) *De la crise financière à la crise systémique*, book in preparation with contributions from Morin, François; Gowan, Peter; and Altvater, Elmar

Amin, Samir and Gunder Frank, André (1985) *N'attendons pas 1984*, Paris, Maspero

Gowan, Peter 'Causing the Credit Crunch: the rise and consequences of the new Wall Street system'

Lordon, Frédéric (2008) *Jusqu'à quand? Pour en finir avec les crises financiers*, Paris, Raisons d'agir

Morin, François (2006) 'La crise financière globalisée et les nouvelles orientations du système', paper presented at the Forum Mondial des Alternatives (FMA), Caracas, Venezuela

2

The contrast between the European and the Chinese historical developments

The general and the particular in the trajectories of humanity's evolution

The concrete, the immediate, is always particular – this is virtually a truism. To stop there would make it impossible to understand the history of humanity. This seems – at the phenomenal level – as if it were composed of a succession of particular trajectories and evolutions, without any connections with each other, except by chance. Each of these successions can only be explained by particular causalities and sequences of events. This method reinforces the tendency towards 'culturalisms', that is, the idea that each people is identified by the specifics of its culture, which are mostly 'transhistoric', in the sense that they persist in spite of change.

Marx is, for me, the key thinker on research into the general, as his research goes beyond the particular. Of course, the general cannot be announced a priori through reflection and idealised reasoning about the essence of phenomena (as Hegel and Auguste Comte would do). It must be inferred from analysis of concrete facts. In such conditions it is clear that there is no absolute guarantee that the proposed induction will be definitive, or even accurate. But such research is obligatory; it cannot be avoided.

When you analyse the particular you will discover how the general makes itself felt through forms of the particular. That is how I read Marx.

With this in mind, I have proposed a reading of historical materialism based on the general succession of three important

2 EUROPEAN AND CHINESE HISTORICAL DEVELOPMENTS

stages in the evolution of human societies: the community stage, the tributary stage and the capitalist stage (potentially overtaken by communism). And I have tried, within this framework, to see in the diversity of the societies at the tributary stage (as in the previous community stage), the particular forms of expression of the general requirements that define each of these stages (see my book (Amin 1981) *Class and Nation*). The proposition goes against the tradition of a banal opposition between the European path (that of the famous five stages – primitive communism, slavery, feudalism, capitalism and socialism, which was not an invention of Stalin but the dominant view in Europe before and after Marx) and the Asian path (or, rather, dead end). The hydraulic thesis, as proposed by Wittfogel, at that time seemed to me overly infantile and mistaken, based on Eurocentric prejudices. My proposition also goes against another tradition, produced by vulgar Marxism, that of the universality of the five stages.

With this also in mind, I proposed looking at the contradictions within the large family of the tributary societies as expressions of a general requirement to go beyond the basic principles of the organisation of a tributary social system by the invention of those that define capitalist modernity (and, beyond, the possibility of socialism/communism). Capitalism was not destined to be Europe's exclusive invention. It was also in the process of developing in the tributary countries of the East, particularly in China, as we shall see later. In my early critique of Eurocentrism, I brought up this very question, which had been ejected from the dominant debate by the discourse on the 'European exception'.

However, once capitalism was constituted in its historic form, that is, starting from Europe, its worldwide expansion through conquest and the submission of other societies to the requirements of its polarising reproduction put an end to the possibility of another path for the capitalist development of humanity (the Chinese path, for example). This expansion destroyed the impact and importance of the variations of local capitalism and involved them all in the dichotomy of the contrast between the dominant capitalist/imperialist centres with the dominated capitalist peripheries, which defines the polarisation peculiar to historical capitalism (European in origin).

I am therefore now proposing a reading of the two paths (that of the Mediterranean/Europe and that of the Chinese world). This is not that of the opposition five stages/Asian dead-end, but is based on another analytical principle that contrasts the full-blown forms of the tributary mode in the Chinese world with the peripheral forms of this same mode in the Mediterranean/European region. The full-blown form in China was visibly strong and stable from its beginnings, while the peripheral forms have always been fragile, resulting in the failure of successive attempts in Europe by the imperial centre to levy tribute, in contrast to its success in the Chinese empire.

Opposition between the European and Chinese development paths: the peasant question

The Mediterranean/European path and the Chinese path diverged right from the beginning. The stability of the full-blown tributary mode involved a solid integration of the peasant world into the overall construction of the system and thus it guaranteed access to land. This choice has been a principle in China from the beginning. There were sometimes serious infringements in its implementation, although they were always overcome. In contrast, in the Mediterranean/Europe region access to land was radically abolished when the principle of private ownership of land was adopted. It became a fundamental and absolute right with the installation of capitalist modernity in its European form.

Historical capitalism, which was the result, then proceeded with the massive expulsion of the rural population and, for many of them, their exclusion from the building of the new society. This involved large-scale emigration, which was made possible by the conquest of the Americas, without which its success would have been impossible. Historical capitalism became a military and conquering imperialist capitalism, involving unprecedented violence.

The path followed by capitalist development in China (before it submitted to the conquering imperialism of the second half of the 19th century) was quite different. It confirmed, instead of abolishing, the access to land by the peasantry as a whole and opted for the intensification of agricultural production and the scattering of industrial manufacturing in the rural regions. This gave China a distinct advantage over Europe in all fields of production. It was lost only later, after the Industrial Revolution had successfully proceeded to shape modern Europe.

Modern China before Europe

European thinkers were aware of the superiority of China, which became the 'model' par excellence, as Etiemble and others recognised. It was a model of administrative rationality: China very early on invented the public service, independent of the aristocracy and the religious clergy, recruiting a state bureaucracy, with competitive entrance examinations. Hundreds of years had to pass before Europe discovered this form of administrative modernity (only in the 19th century), which was gradually imitated by the rest of the world. China was a model of rationality in the way it implemented advanced technologies for agricultural and artisanal/manufacturing production. This admiration for the Chinese model only disappeared when the Europeans succeeded, through their military superiority (and by that alone), in breaking the Chinese model.

China was therefore engaged on the path of inventing capitalism along lines that would have been very different from those of the conquering globalised imperialist capitalism.

Why did the modern Chinese path, the beginnings of which predated that of Europe by at least 500 years, not take off? And why did the European path, which started later, take definite shape in a short space of time and then become able to impose itself at the world level? My effort in trying to explain this is based on an emphasis of the advantages of the European tributary societies on the periphery (the feudal path) as opposed to the inertia imposed by the solidity of the central form of the Chinese tributary mode. This is a more general expression of what I have described as unequal development: the peripheral forms, because they were less solid and more adaptable, made it easier to overtake the contradictions of the old system, while the centralised forms, which were more solid, slowed the movement down.

Premodern regionalisations and the centralisation of tributary surplus

Nowadays the term globalisation is used in various ways, often vague and ambiguous. Moreover, the phenomenon in itself is considered as a given and unavoidable, an expression of the evolution of reality that is claimed to be ineluctable. Phenomena similar to modern globalisation – which for the first time in history concerns the entire world – are to be found in more ancient times. However, these only concerned the large regions of the Old World, the so-called pre-Colombian Americas being isolated and unknown by the former (and the former unknown to the latter). I will call these globalisations regionalisations.

I describe all these phenomena with one common criterion, that of organising command over the surplus of current production at the level of the whole region (or of its world) by a central authority and the extent of centralisation over that surplus used by that authority. This in turn regulated the sharing of access to the surplus that it commanded.

The regionalisations (or globalisation) concerned could be inclined towards homogeneity or polarisation, according to whether the redistribution of the surplus was subjected to laws and customs that aimed expressly at one or other of these objectives, or they could be produced by deploying their own logic.

The centralisation of tributary surplus

In all the premodern systems (the old regionalisations) this surplus appears as a tribute, and in the modern (capitalist) system as profit for capital or, more precisely, the rent of dominant oligopolistic capital. The specific difference between these two forms of surplus is qualitative and decisive. Levying tributary surplus is transparent; it is the free work of the subjugated peasants on the land of the nobles and a proportion of the harvest creamed off by the latter or by the state. These are quite natural, non-monetary forms and even when they assume a monetary form it is generally marginal or exceptional. The levying of profit or rent by dominant capital is, in contrast, opaque as it results from the way the network of trade in monetised goods operates: wages of workers,

2 EUROPEAN AND CHINESE HISTORICAL DEVELOPMENTS

purchases and sales of the means of production and the results of economic activities.

Taxation of tributary surplus is thus inseparable from the exercise of political power in the region (large or small) where it operates. In contrast, that of capitalist surplus appears to be dissociated from the exercise of political power, apparently being the product of the mechanisms that control the markets (of labour, products and capital itself). The (premodern) tributary systems were not applied over vast territories and large numbers of people. The level of development of the productive forces typical of these ancient times was still limited and the surplus consisted essentially of what was produced by the peasant communities. The tributary societies could be split up, sometimes to the extreme, with each village or seigneury (domain of a feudal lord) constituting an elementary society.

The fragmentation of tributary societies did not exclude them from participating in broader trade networks, commercial or otherwise, or in systems of power extending over greater areas. Elementary tributary systems were not necessarily autarchic, even if most of their production had to ensure their own reproduction without outside support.

The emergence of tributary empires has always required a political power capable of imposing itself on the scattered tributary societies. Among those in this category were the Roman, Caliphal and Ottoman empires in the Europe/Mediterranean/Middle East region, the Chinese empire and the imperial states that India experienced on various occasions during its history. This emergence of tributary empires in turn facilitated the expansion of commercial and monetary relationships within them and in their external relations.

The tributary empires did not necessarily pursue the political aim of the homogenisation of conditions in the region controlled by central power. But the laws and their usages governing these systems, dominated by the political authorities to which the functioning of the economy remained subordinated, did not in themselves create a growing polarisation between the subregions constituting the empire.

History has largely proven the fragility of tributary empires whose apogee was short – a few centuries – followed by long periods of disintegration, usually described as decadence. The reason for this fragility is that the centralisation of the surplus was not based on the internal requirement necessary for the reproduction of elementary tributary societies. They were very vulnerable to attack from outside and revolts from within by the dominated classes or provinces, such as they were. Evolutions in the different fields of ecology, demography, military armaments and the trade in goods over long distances proved to be strong enough to turn this vulnerability into a catastrophe.

The only exception – a vital one – was that of the Chinese empire.

The Chinese itinerary: a long, calm river?

The preceding reflections concentrated on the Middle East/Mediterranean/Europe region. This region was the scene of the formation of the first (tributary) civilisations – Egypt and Mesopotamia – and, later, of its Greek market/slavery periphery. Then, as from the Hellenistic period, it saw successive attempts to construct tributary empires (Roman, Byzantine, Caliphal, Ottoman). These were never really able to become stable and they experienced long and chaotic declines. Perhaps for this reason conditions were more favourable to the early emergence of capitalism in its historical form, as a prelude to the conquest of the world by Europe.

The itinerary of China was extremely different. Almost from the start it became a tributary empire that was exceptionally stable, in spite of moments when it threatened to fall apart. Nevertheless these threats were always finally overcome.

Phonetic writing, conceptual writing

There are various reasons for the success of the construction of tributary centralisation throughout the Chinese world. Chinese authors, who are not very well known outside their country (such as Wen Tiejun), have proposed different hypotheses, depending on the geography and ecology of their region. They emphasise the early invention of intensive agriculture, associated with a population density that gradually became considerably greater than that of the Mediterranean/European world. It is not our purpose

2 EUROPEAN AND CHINESE HISTORICAL DEVELOPMENTS

here to open up a debate on these difficult questions, which have been barely studied up until now because of the dominance of Eurocentrism. Personally, I would insist on the very long-term effects of the Chinese adoption of conceptual writing.

Phonetic writing (alphabetical or syllabic), invented in the Middle East, gradually became the basis of all the languages of the Mediterranean/European region and the Indian subcontinent. It is only understandable by those who know the meaning of the words as they are pronounced in the spoken language, and it requires translation for others. The expansion of this way of writing reinforced the differences between the languages and consequently the forms of identity that were based upon them. This constituted an obstacle to the expansion of regional political powers and therefore to tributary centralisation. Then, with capitalist modernity it created the mythology of a nation/state that was linguistically homogenous. This persists – and is even reinforced – in contemporary Europe and is thus an obstacle to its political unification. The obstacle can only (partially) be overcome by adopting a common language, foreign for many, whether it is the languages of the empires inherited by modern states (English, French and Portuguese in Africa, English in India and up to a point Spanish and Portuguese for the Amerindians of Latin America), or the 'business English' that has become the language of contemporary Europe.

The Chinese invented another way of writing which was conceptual and not phonetic. The same character described an object (like a door) or an idea (such as friendship) and can be read with a different pronunciation, for example, 'door' or *'bab'*, 'friendship' or *'sadaka'* by readers who are respectively English or Arab. This form of writing was an important factor in promoting the expansion of the imperial power of the Chinese world at the continental level. It was a world whose population was comparable to that of all the Americas from Alaska to Tierra del Fuego in Argentina and of Europe from Portugal to Vladivostok. The conceptual way of Chinese writing enabled the reading of one text in all the different languages of the subcontinent. And it is only recently that, through generalised education, the Mandarin language of Beijing has started to become the (phonetic) language of the whole Chinese world.

China was five centuries ahead of Europe

The image of the Chinese trajectory as being the course of a 'long, calm river' is certainly somewhat forced.

Ancient China, until the introduction of Buddhism in the first centuries of the Christian era, was made up of multiple tributary formations, organised in principalities and kingdoms that were often in conflict. There was, nevertheless, a tendency towards unifying them into one single empire, which had its early expression in the writings of Confucius 500 hundred years before Jesus Christ, in the Warring States period.

The Chinese world then adopted a religion of individual salvation, Buddhism – although it was mixed with Taoism – following the example of Christian Europe. The two societies – feudal, Christian Europe and imperial, Buddhist China – had striking similarities. But there were also important differences: China was a unified political empire which rose to remarkable heights under the Tang dynasty, while feudal Europe never achieved this. The tendency to reconstitute the right of access to land each time that it seriously deteriorated in China contrasted with the long-lasting fragmentation of European feudal property.

China freed itself from religion, in this case Buddhism, from the Song period and definitively with the Ming. It therefore entered into modernity some five centuries before the European renaissance. The analogy between the Chinese renaissance and the later European one is impressive. The Chinese 'returned to their roots' of Confucianism in a free, rational and non-religious reinterpretation, like that of a European renaissance which invented a Greco-Roman ancestor to break with what the Enlightenment described as the religious obscurantism of the Middle Ages.

All the conditions were then met to enable the modern Chinese world to accomplish remarkable progress in all fields: the organisation of the state, scientific knowledge, agricultural and manufacturing production techniques and rational thinking. China invented secularism 500 years before it developed in Europe. Modern China put forward the idea that it was man who made history, a notion which later became a central theme of the Enlightenment. The impact of this progress was reinforced by the periodic correction of dangerous drifts (see Translator's note) towards the private appropriation of land.

2 EUROPEAN AND CHINESE HISTORICAL DEVELOPMENTS

The stability of the economic and political organisation of China constituted a model for the development of productive forces based on the continued intensification of agricultural production, which was in striking contrast with the model of historical European capitalism based on the private appropriation of agrarian land, the expulsion of the rural population, massive emigration and the conquest of the world associated with it. This model of European capitalism was that of accumulation by dispossession, not only primitive but permanent (the other aspect of the polarisation inherent in capitalist globalisation). China was launched on a path that could have led to a capitalism of a different kind, closed up on itself rather than conquering. The prodigious expansion of commercial relations associated with the levying of tribute and not separated from it shows that this possibility did exist. But this association made the evolutionary process relatively slow compared with that of a Europe in transition towards full-blown capitalism.

For this reason China kept its advantage – in terms of the average productivity of social labour – over Europe until the Industrial Revolution of the 19th century.

As I said before, the Enlightenment in Europe recognised this advance of China, which it saw as a model. However, neither the Europe of the Enlightenment of the mercantilist transition period, nor, later on, the Europe of the full-blown capitalism of the 19th century managed to overcome the fragmentation of the kingdoms of the ancien régime, then of the modern nation states, to create a unified power capable of controlling the centralisation of the surplus tribute, then capitalist surplus, as China had done.

For their part, Chinese observers clearly saw the advantage of their historic development. A Chinese traveller, visiting Europe in the aftermath of the Franco-Prussian war of 1870, compared the state of the continent to that of the Warring States, 500 years before Jesus Christ.

The decline of China, caused by a combination of the exhaustion of the model of the intensification/commercialisation of agricultural and rural production, together with European military aggression, was relatively short. It did not cause the break-up of this continental state, although the threat was apparent during the decline. Some of the essential characteristics of the Chinese

Revolution and of the path it took after its victory in the successive Maoist and post-Maoist moments should be seen in this perspective of an exceptionally long duration.

3

Historical capitalism – accumulation by dispossession

Dominant bourgeois thought has replaced the historical reality of capitalism with an imaginary construction based on the principle – claimed to be eternal – of the rational and egoistical behaviour of the individual. 'Rational' society – produced by the competition required by this principle – is thus seen as having arrived at the end of history. Conventional economics, which is the fundamental base of this thinking, therefore substitutes the generalised market for the reality of capitalism (and the capitalist market).

Marxist thought has been built up based on quite another vision, that of the permanent transformation of the fundamental structures of societies, which is always historical.

In this framework – that of historical materialism – capitalism is historical, has had a beginning and will have an end. Accepting this principle, the nature of this historical capitalism should be the object of continual reflection, which is not always the case in the ranks of the 'historical Marxisms' (that is, Marxism as interpreted by those who claim it). Certainly one can accept the very general idea that capitalism constitutes a necessary stage, preparing conditions for socialism – a more advanced stage of human civilisation. But this idea is too general and insufficient precisely because it reduces 'capitalism – necessary stage' to actually existing (see Translator's note) historical capitalism.

I shall sum up my reflections on this question in the following points to be developed over subsequent pages:

- Accumulation through dispossession is a permanent feature in the history of capitalism.
- Historical capitalism is, therefore, imperialist by nature at all stages of its development, in the sense that it polarises owing to the inherent effect of the laws that govern it.

- From this it follows that this capitalism cannot become the unavoidable stage for the peoples of the peripheries of the historical capitalist system. Therefore, this stage is not necessary to create, here as elsewhere (in the centres of the system), the conditions for overtaking it by socialism. Development and underdevelopment are the two inseparable sides of the historical capitalist coin.
- This historical capitalism is itself inseparable from the European conquest of the world. It is inseparable from the Eurocentric ideology which is, by definition, a non-universal form of civilisation.
- Other forms of response to the need for accelerated accumulation (compared with the rhythms of the accumulation of the ancient epochs of civilisation) – a necessary premise for the socialism of the future – would have been possible. This can be discussed. But these forms, perhaps more visible in an embryonic way elsewhere than in the Europe of the transition to capitalism (in China, among others), have not been implemented because they have been crushed by the European conquest.
- Thus there is no alternative for human civilisation other than to engage in a construction of socialism, this in turn being based on the strategic concepts that must command the objective results produced by the globalised and polarising expansion of western capitalism/imperialism.

Accumulation by dispossession: a permanent historical feature of actually existing capitalism

The vulgar (see Translator's note) ideology of conventional economics and the cultural and social thinking that goes with it claim that accumulation is financed by the virtuous savings of the rich (the wealthy owners), like nations. History hardly confirms this invention of Anglo-American puritans. It is, on the contrary, an accumulation largely financed by the dispossession of some (the majority) for the profit of others (the minority). Marx rigorously analysed these processes, which he described as primitive accumulation, with the dispossession of the English peasants (the enclosures), that of the Irish peasants (for the benefit of the conquering English landlords) and that of American colonisation being eloquent examples. In reality, this primitive accumulation

3 HISTORICAL CAPITALISM – ACCUMULATION BY DISPOSSESSION

has not exclusively taken place in bygone and outdated capitalism. It continues today.

It is possible to measure the importance of this 'accumulation through dispossession', an expression I prefer to that of primitive accumulation. The measure that I am proposing here is based on the consequences of this dispossession, and can be expressed in demographic terms and in terms of the apparent value of the social results that accompany it.

The population of the world tripled between 1500 (450–550 million inhabitants) and 1900 (1,600 million), reaching three and a quarter times the 1500 population during the 20th century (at over 6,000 million). But the proportion of Europeans (those of Europe and of their conquered territories in America, South Africa, Australia and New Zealand) increased from 18 per cent (at most) in 1500 to 37 per cent in 1900, before falling gradually during the 20th century. The first four centuries (1500 to 1900) correspond to the European conquest of the world, and the 20th century – which continues through to the 21st century – to the awakening of the South and the renaissance of the conquered peoples.

The European conquest of the world constituted the colossal dispossession of the Amerindians of the Americas, who lost their land and natural resources to the colonists. The Amerindians were almost totally exterminated (through a genocide in North America) or reduced, by the effects of this dispossession and their over-exploitation by the Spanish and Portuguese conquerors, to one-tenth of their former population. The slave trade that followed represented a plunder of a large part of Africa, setting back the progress of the continent by half a millennium. Such phenomena are visible in South Africa, Zimbabwe, Kenya and Algeria, and still more in Australia and New Zealand. This accumulation by dispossession characterises the state of Israel, which is a colonisation still in progress. No less visible are the consequences of colonial exploitation among the peasantry subjected by British India, or in the Dutch Indies, the Philippines or Africa, as evinced by famines (the famous famine of Bengal, those of contemporary Africa). The method was inaugurated by the English in Ireland, the population of which – formerly the same as that of England – today only represents one-tenth of that of the English, caused largely by the organised famine denounced by Marx.

Dispossession not only affected the peasant populations, which were the great majority of peoples in the past. It also destroyed the capacity for industrial production (artisan and manufacturing) of regions that for a long time had been more prosperous than Europe itself: China, India and others (indisputable proof of which is described by Amiya Kumar Bagchi (2005) in his latest work, *Perilous Passage*).

It is important here to understand that this destruction was not produced by the laws of the market, with European industry – claiming to be more effective – having taken the place of non-competitive production. The ideological discourse does not discuss the political and military violence utilised to achieve this destruction. It was not the canons of English industry, but the cannons of the gunboat period, which won out in spite of the superiority – not inferiority – of the Chinese and Indian industries. Industrialisation, which was prohibited by the colonial administration, did the rest and 'developed the underdevelopment' of Asia and Africa during the 19th and 20th centuries. The colonial atrocities and the extreme exploitation of workers were the natural means and results of accumulation through dispossession.

From 1500 to 1800, the material production of the European centres progressed at a rate that was hardly greater than that of its demographic growth (but this was strong in relative terms for that era). These rhythms accelerated during the 19th century, with the deepening – and not the attenuation – of the exploitation of peoples overseas, which is why I speak of the permanent accumulation by dispossession and not primitive (i.e. first, preceding) accumulation. This does not exclude the fact that the contribution of accumulation financed by technological progress during the 19th and 20th centuries – the successive industrial revolutions – then took on an importance that it never had during the three mercantilist centuries that preceded it. Finally, therefore, from 1500 to 1900 the apparent production of the new centres of the capitalist/imperialist world system (western and central Europe, the United States and, a late arrival, Japan) increased by seven to seven and a half times, in contrast with that of the peripheries, which barely doubled. The gap widened as had never been possible in the history of all humanity. During the course of the 20th century, it widened still further, bringing apparent per capita

3 HISTORICAL CAPITALISM – ACCUMULATION BY DISPOSSESSION

incomes in the centres to a level 15 to 20 times greater than that of the peripheries as a whole.

The accumulation by dispossession of centuries of mercantilism had largely financed the luxuries and standard of living of the governing classes of the period (the Ancien Régime), without benefiting the popular classes (see Translator's note) whose standard of living often worsened as they were themselves victims of the accumulation by dispossession of large swathes of the peasantry. But, above all, it had financed an extraordinary reinforcement of the powers of the modern state, of its administration and its military power. This can be seen in the wars of the French Revolution and of the empire, which marked the juncture between the preceding mercantilist epoch and the subsequent industrialisation period. This accumulation is therefore at the origin of the two major transformations that had taken place by the 19th century: the first Industrial Revolution and the easy colonial conquest.

The popular classes did not benefit from the colonial prosperity at first, not in fact until late in the 19th century. This was obvious in the tragic scenes of the destitution of workers in England, as described by Engels. But they had an escape route, the massive emigration that accelerated in the 19th and 20th centuries, to the point that the population of European origin became greater than that of the regions to which they emigrated. Is it possible to imagine two or three billion Asians and Africans having that advantage today?

The 19th century represented the apogee of this system of capitalist/imperialist globalisation. In fact, from this point on the expansion of capitalism and westernisation, in the brutal sense of the term, made it impossible to distinguish between the economic dimension of the conquest and its cultural dimension, Eurocentrism.

The various forms of external and internal colonialisms which I refer to here (for more details, see Amin (2010), p. 108 onwards) constituted the framework of accumulation by dispossession and gave substance to imperialist rent, the effects of which proved decisive in shaping the rich societies of the contemporary imperialist centre.

Capitalism: a parenthesis in history

The development of historical capitalism was based on the private appropriation of agrarian land, the subordination of agricultural production to the requirements of the market and, on this basis, the continuing and accelerating expulsion of the peasant population for the benefit of a small number of capitalist farmers, who were no longer peasants and who ended up forming an insignificant percentage of the population (from 5 to 10 per cent). They were, however, capable of producing enough to feed (well) all their countries' population, and even export much of the surplus production. This path, started by England in the 18th century (with the enclosures) and gradually extended to the rest of Europe in the 19th century, constituted the essence of the historical path of capitalist development.

It seemed very effective. But whether it is effective or not, can it be imitated today in the peripheries of the system?

This capitalist path was only possible because the Europeans had at their disposal the great safety valve of immigration to the Americas, which we mentioned earlier. But this solution simply does not exist for the peoples of the periphery today. Moreover, modern industrialisation cannot absorb more than a small minority of the rural populations concerned because, compared with the industries of the 19th century, it now integrates technological progress – the condition of its efficiency – which economises the labour that it employs. The capitalist path cannot produce anything else than a 'slum planet' (which is visible in the contemporary capitalist Third World), producing and reproducing indefinitely cheap labour. This is the reason why this path is politically unfeasible. In Europe, North America and Japan, the capitalist path – involving emigration outlets and the profits from imperialism – certainly created, rather belatedly, the conditions for a social compromise between capital and labour (particularly apparent in the period following the Second World War, with the welfare state, although this had already existed in less explicit forms since the end of the 19th century). The conditions of a compromise based on this model do not exist for the peripheries of today. The capitalist path in China and Vietnam, for example, cannot create a broad popular alliance, integrating the worker class and the peasantry.

3 HISTORICAL CAPITALISM – ACCUMULATION BY DISPOSSESSION

It can only find its social basis in the new middle classes that have become the exclusive beneficiaries of this development. The social-democratic way is now therefore excluded. The inevitable alternative is one of a peasant development model, to which we shall return in Chapter 5.

The question of natural resources constitutes a second decisive issue in the conflict of civilisation that opposes capitalism to socialism in the future. The exploitation of the non-renewable resources of the South for the exclusive profit of the wasteful consumption of the North is also a form of accumulation by dispossession. The exchange of these resources against renewable goods and services jeopardises the future of the peoples of the South, who are being sacrificed on the altar of the super-profits of the imperialist oligopolies.

The destructive dimension of capitalism, at least for the peoples of the peripheries, makes it impossible to believe that this system can be sustainable and imitated by those who seem to be backward. Its place in the history of humanity is that of a parenthesis, one which creates the conditions for overtaking it. If this does not happen capitalism can only lead to barbarism and the end of all human civilisation.

The course of actually existing capitalism has been composed of a long period of maturation lasting several centuries and leading to a short apogee (the 19th century), followed by a probable long decline beginning in the 20th century, which could initiate a long transition to globalised socialism.

Capitalism was not the result of a brutal, almost magical apparition, chosen by the London/Amsterdam/Paris triangle and established in the short period of the Reformation/Renaissance of the 16th century. Three centuries earlier, it had experienced its first formulation in the Italian cities. The first formulas were brilliant but limited in space and thus crushed by the surrounding feudal European world. This is why, having been set back by successive defeats, these first experiences collapsed. It is also possible to discuss various antecedents to these in the commercial towns along the silk route of China and India to the Arab and Persian Islamic Middle East (see my comments on the Chinese path described in Chapter 2). Later, in 1492, with the conquest of the Americas by the Spanish and the Portuguese, began the creation of the mercantile/

slavery/capitalist system. But the monarchies of Madrid and Lisbon, for various reasons which I shall not go into here, were unable to give a definitive form to mercantilism which, instead, the English, Dutch and French were to invent. This third wave of social, economic, political and cultural transformations, which was to produce the transition to capitalism in its historical form that we know (the Ancien Régime) would have been unthinkable without the two preceding waves. Why should it not be the same for socialism, a long process, lasting centuries, for the invention of a more advanced stage of human civilisation?

The apogee of the system did not last long. Hardly one century separated the Industrial and French Revolutions from 1917. This was the century when these two revolutions were accomplished, taking over Europe and its North American offspring – as well as the challenges to them, from the Commune of Paris in 1871 to the 1917 revolution – and achieving the conquest of the world, which seemed resigned to its fate.

Could this historical capitalism continue to develop, allowing the peripheries of the system to overcome their backwardness to become developed capitalist societies like those in the dominant centres? If this were possible, if the laws of the system allowed it, then the catching-up by and through capitalism would have had an objective unavoidable strength, a necessary precondition to an ultimate socialism. But this vision, obvious and dominant as it seemed, was simply false. Historical capitalism is – and continues to be – polarising by nature, rendering catching-up impossible.

Historical capitalism must be overtaken and this cannot be done unless the societies in the peripheries (the great majority of humanity) set to work out systematic strategies of delinking from the global system and reconstructing themselves on an autonomous basis, thus creating the conditions for an alternative globalisation, engaged on the long road to world socialism. I will not take up this analysis here, as it can be read in my *Obsolescent Capitalism* (Amin 2003, Annex IV). Pursuing the capitalist path to development thus represents, for the peoples of the periphery, a tragic impasse. This is because the developed capitalism of some – the dominant minority centres (20 per cent of the world population) – requires the underdevelopment of the others (80 per cent

3 HISTORICAL CAPITALISM – ACCUMULATION BY DISPOSSESSION

of the world's population). The impasse can thus be seen in all dimensions of social, economic and political life. And it manifests itself most strikingly in the agrarian question.

The 20th century: the first wave of socialist revolutions and the awakening of the South

Thus the apogee of the system lasted only a short while, hardly a century in fact. The 20th century experienced the first wave of the great revolutions conducted in the name of socialism (Russia, China, Vietnam, Cuba) and the radicalisation of the liberation struggles of Asia, Africa and Latin America (the peripheries of the imperialist/capitalist system) whose ambitions were expressed in the Bandung project (1955–80).

This coincidence was not by chance. The globalisation of capitalism/imperialism had imposed the greatest tragedy in human history on the peoples of the peripheries concerned, showing up the destructive character of capital accumulation. The law of pauperisation formulated by Marx at the level of the system was still more violent than the father of socialist thought had imagined. This page of history has been turned over for good. The peoples of the periphery will no longer accept the destiny that capitalism reserves for them. This change of fundamental attitudes is irreversible. It means that capitalism has entered into its decline. This does not exclude various illusions: those of reforms capable of giving capitalism a human face (which it has never had for the majority of peoples); those of a possible catching-up in the system, which is cherished by the governing classes in the emerging countries, exhilarated by momentary success; and those of nostalgic retreat (para-religious or para-ethnic) into which many of the excluded peoples have sunk at the moment. These illusions continue as we are still in the trough of the wave. The wave of the revolutions of the 20th century is spent and that of the new radicalism of the 21st century has not yet affirmed itself. And in an interregnum, 'a great variety of morbid symptoms appear', as Gramsci wrote. The awakening of the peoples of the periphery has made itself felt since the 20th century, not only because of their demographic catch-up, but also by their express desire to reconstruct their states and their society, delinked from the imperialism of the four preceding centuries.

I therefore proposed looking at the 20th century as one of the first wave of struggles for the emancipation of the workers and of peoples (Amin 2008, Chapter 1), of which I mention here only the main theses.

Bandung and the first globalisation of the struggles (1955–80)

The governments and peoples of Asia and Africa proclaimed at Bandung, in 1955, their desire to reconstruct the world system on a basis of recognising the rights of nations that had up until then been dominated. This 'right to development' was the foundation of globalisation at that time, implemented in a multipolar negotiated framework imposed on an imperialism that was forced to adjust to these new requirements.

The industrialisation progress that started during the Bandung era was not the result of imperialist logic but was imposed by the victories of the peoples of the South. Undoubtedly, this progress cherished the illusion of 'catching-up', which seemed on the way to becoming a reality, while imperialism, forced to adjust to the demands of the development of the peripheries, recomposed itself around new forms of domination. The old contrast of imperialist countries/dominated countries, which was synonymous with the contrast of the industrialised countries/non-industrialised countries, gradually gave way to a new contrast based on the centralisation of the advantages associated with the five new monopolies of the imperialist centres (control over new technologies, natural resources, the global financial system, communications and weapons of mass destruction).

The long decline of capitalism and the long transition to world socialism

Is the long decline of capitalism the same as the long positive transition to socialism? If it is to be so, it is necessary that the 21st century prolongs the 20th century and radicalises the objectives of social transformation. This is completely possible, but the conditions must be spelt out, otherwise the long decline of capitalism will turn into the continual degradation of human civilisation. I shall refer here to what I wrote on this subject more than 25 years

3 HISTORICAL CAPITALISM – ACCUMULATION BY DISPOSSESSION

ago, in 'Revolution or decadence?', a chapter in my book *Class and Nation* (Amin 1981).

The decline was not a continuous, linear process. There were moments of revival, of the counteroffensive of capital, like the counteroffensive of the governing classes of the Ancien Régime on the eve of the French Revolution.

The present time is of that kind. The 20th century was a first chapter in the long apprenticeship of the people in going beyond capitalism and inventing new socialist forms of living, to borrow the expression of Domenico Losurdo. Like him, I do not analyse its development in terms of a failure (of socialism, of national independence), as reactionary propaganda – which has the wind in its sails today – tries to make out. On the contrary, it is the very successes and not the failures of this first wave of socialist and national popular experiences which are at the origin of the problems of the contemporary world. I have analysed the projects of this first wave in terms of three families of social and political advances: the welfare state in the imperialist West (the historical compromise between capital and labour of the period), the actually existing socialisms (Soviet and Maoist) and the national popular systems of the Bandung era. The analysis is made in terms of their complementarity and conflictuality at the world level (a different perspective from that of the cold war and the bipolarity proposed today by the defenders of the capitalist end of history school, as I stress the multipolar character of globalisation in the 20th century). The social contradictions of each of these systems and the tentative nature of these first advances explain their loss of impetus and finally their defeat, and not their failure (Amin 2003, pp. 7–21).

It is thus this inertia that created favourable conditions for the current capitalist counteroffensive, the new perilous passage of the liberations of the 20th century to those of the 21st century. It is therefore important to now tackle the nature of this trough moment that separates the two centuries and to identify the new challenges that confront the peoples of the world.

ENDING THE CRISIS OF CAPITALISM OR ENDING CAPITALISM?

The counteroffensive of capitalism in decline

The contrast of centres and peripheries is no longer similar to that of industrialised countries and non-industrialised countries. The polarisation of centres/peripheries, which gave the expansion of world capitalism its imperialist character, continues and even increases through the 'five new monopolies' that the imperialist centres enjoy. In these conditions, the pursuit of accelerated development by the emerging peripheries, implemented with unquestioned success (in China, particularly, but also in other countries of the South) has not eradicated imperialist domination. It has led to a new contrast between the centres and the peripheries, not to its overtaking.

Imperialism is no longer written in the plural – as in the earlier phases of its development – it is a collective imperialism of the Triad (the United States, Europe, Japan). In this sense, the common interests shared by the oligopolies based in the Triad are greater than the conflicts of (mercantile) interests that might cause them to oppose each other. This collective character of imperialism is expressed through the management of a world system by the common instruments of the Triad: at the economic level, by the World Trade Organisation (the colonial ministry of the Triad), the International Monetary Fund (the colonial collective monetary agency), the World Bank (the propaganda ministry), the Organisation for Economic Cooperation and Development (OECD) and the European Union (constituted to prevent Europe from extricating itself from liberalism); and at the political level, by the G7/G8, the armed forces of the United States and their subordinate instrument, NATO (North Atlantic Treaty Organisation) (with the marginalisation/domestication of the United Nations completing the picture). The US hegemonic project, implemented through a programme of the military control of the planet (involving, among other things, the abrogation of international law and the law that Washington has conferred upon itself to conduct the preventive wars of its choice), is articulated through collective imperialism and makes it possible for the American leader to overcompensate for its economic deficiencies.

3 HISTORICAL CAPITALISM – ACCUMULATION BY DISPOSSESSION

What strategy to construct convergence in diversity?

The peoples of the three continents (Asia, Africa and Latin America) are confronted today with the expansion of the imperialist system called globalised neoliberalism, which is nothing less than the construction of apartheid at the world level. The new imperial order will be challenged, but by whom? And what will result from this challenge?

Here I shall outline the main proposals that I have developed elsewhere (*From Capitalism to Civilization* (2010), p. 127 onwards).

There is no doubt that the image of the dominant reality makes it difficult to imagine an immediate challenge to this order. The governing classes of the countries of the South, defeated as they are, have largely accepted playing their role of subordinate comprador classes while the peoples, confused and caught up in the daily struggle for survival, often seem to accept their lot or even, worse still, to harbour new illusions that their own governing classes hold out before them.

The governing classes of certain countries of the South have obviously chosen a strategy that is neither that of passive submission to the dominant forces in the world system nor of declared opposition to them: a strategy of active interventions upon which they base their hopes to accelerate the development of their country. China – owing to the solidity of its national construction given to it by its revolution and Maoism, its option to conserve control of its currency and capital movements and its refusal to question the collective ownership of the land (the main revolutionary conquest of the peasants) – is better equipped than the others to make this choice and to achieve incontestably brilliant results.

Can this experience continue? And what are its limits? After analysing the contradictions inherent in this option I have concluded that the idea of a national capitalism capable of imposing itself on equal terms with the main powers of the world system is based largely on illusions. The objective conditions inherited from history do not make it possible to implement a social compromise between capital, labour and the peasantry that would guarantee the stability of the system. In time the social compromise has to drift (see Translator's note) to the right (and then be confronted by the growing social movements of the popular classes), or evolve towards the left by building market socialism as a stage along the long transition to socialism. The problems of Vietnam are similar. The apparently analogous choices made by the governing classes of the other so-called emerging countries are still more fragile. Neither Brazil nor India – because they have not had a radical revolution like China – are capable of posing strong resistance to the double pressures of imperialism and the reactionary local classes.

And yet the societies of the South – at least some of them – are today equipped with the means to enable them to completely rid themselves of the monopolies of the imperialist centres. These societies are capable of developing by themselves without falling into dependency. They have the potential of a technological mastery that would enable them to use technology for themselves. They can constrain the North, recover the use of their natural resources and force the North to adjust to a consumption pattern that is less scandalous. They can extricate themselves from financial globalisation. Already they are questioning the monopoly on weapons of mass destruction that the United States wants to reserve for itself. They can develop South–South trade (in goods, services, capital, technologies), something which was unthinkable in 1955 when none of these countries possessed industries and the mastery of technology. More than ever before, the possibility of delinking is on the agenda.

Will these societies do it? And who will undertake it, the existing governing bourgeois classes? I very much doubt it. Will it be the popular classes in power? In all probability, the first will be national/popular transitional regimes.

The inseparable capitalism/socialism and North/South conflicts

The North/South (centres/peripheries) conflict is a major issue in the whole history of capitalist development. It is the reason why the struggle of the peoples of the South for their liberation – which in general is proving victorious – is based on a questioning of capitalism. This is inevitable. The capitalism/socialism conflicts and those of the North/South are inseparable. Socialism

3 HISTORICAL CAPITALISM – ACCUMULATION BY DISPOSSESSION

is inconceivable without the universalism that involves the equality of peoples. Here again I refer the reader to the proposals that I developed in *From Capitalism to Civilization*.

Capitalism is a world system and not just the juxtaposing of national capitalist systems, and so political and social struggles, if they are to be effective, must be conducted simultaneously in the national arena (which remains decisive because the conflicts, alliances and social and political compromises are to be worked out there) and at the world level. This viewpoint, which is obvious to me, seems to have been that of Marx and the historical Marxisms ('Workers of the world, unite!') and, in its enriched Maoist version, 'Proletarians of all countries, oppressed peoples, unite!'

It is impossible to foresee the trajectory that will be traced by the unequal advances of the struggles in the South and in the North. My feeling is that at this moment the South is going through a crisis, but that it is a crisis of growth, in the sense that the pursuit of the liberation objectives of its peoples is irreversible. The peoples of the North would do well to take their measure, or better still adopt the same perspective and associate it with the construction of socialism. There was a moment of solidarity of this kind at the time of Bandung: young Europeans proclaimed their solidarity with the Third World. It was doubtlessly naive, but how much better than their current turning in on themselves.

Without going back to the analyses of actually existing world capitalism that I have developed elsewhere, I will just recall their conclusions. In my opinion, humanity cannot engage seriously in the construction of a socialist alternative to capitalism unless things change in the developed West. That does not mean at all that the peoples of the periphery have to wait for this change and, until it happens, content themselves with adapting to the possibilities offered by capitalist globalisation. On the contrary, it is more probable that, to the extent that things begin to change in the peripheries, the western societies, forced into it, could be led, in their turn, to evolve as required for the progress of humanity as a whole. If this does not happen, the worst is most probable: barbarism and the suicide of human civilisation. Of course, I envisage the desirable and possible changes in both the centres and in the peripheries of the global system in the framework of what I have called 'the long transition'.

In the peripheries of globalised capitalism – by definition the storm zones in the imperialist system – a form of revolution certainly remains on the agenda. But its aim is by nature ambiguous and vague – national liberation from imperialism (and the maintenance of much of, or even all of, the essence of the social relationships that underpin capitalist modernity) – or will it be more than that? Whether it was the radical revolutions of China, Vietnam and Cuba or those which were not radical elsewhere in Asia, Africa and Latin America, the challenge remained to catch up and/or do something else. This challenge was in turn linked to another task generally considered of equal priority: to defend the Soviet Union, which was being encircled. The Soviet Union and later China found themselves confronted by the strategies of systematic isolation used by dominant capitalism and the western powers. One can therefore understand why, revolution not being on the immediate agenda elsewhere, priority was generally given to saving the post-revolutionary states.

The Soviet Union and China experienced the vicissitudes of the great revolutions and also had to confront the consequences of the unequal expansion of world capitalism. Both these factors gradually sacrificed the original communist objectives to the immediate requirements of an economic catching-up. This shift, abandoning the aim of social ownership by which the communism of Marx defined itself, instead substituted state management. This was accompanied by the decline of popular democracy, which was crushed by a brutal (and sometimes bloody) dictatorship of the post-revolutionary power, accelerating an evolution towards the restoration of capitalism. In both experiences, priority was given to the defence of the post-revolutionary state and internal means were used for this purpose, as well as external strategies giving priority to such a defence. The communist parties were thus invited to fall in line with this option, not only with respect to the global strategic direction but also in their tactical day-to-day adjustments. This inevitably caused a rapid weakening of critical thinking among the revolutionaries, whose abstract discourse on the 'revolution' (always 'imminent') was far removed from an analysis of the real contradictions of society, something supported by maintaining almost military forms of organisation against all odds.

3 HISTORICAL CAPITALISM – ACCUMULATION BY DISPOSSESSION

Those of the avant garde who refused to align themselves, and sometimes dared to face the reality of post-revolutionary societies, nevertheless did not renounce the original Leninist hypothesis (the 'imminent revolution'), without taking into account that this was clearly refuted by the facts. Thus there was Trotskyism and the parties of the Fourth International. Then there were a good number of organisations of activist revolutionaries, inspired by Maoism or by Guevarism. Examples of this are numerous, from the Philippines to India (the Naxalites), from the Arab world (with the nationalist/communist Arabs – the Qawmiyin – and those emulating them in South Yemen) to Latin America (Guevarism).

The great national liberation movements in Asia and in Africa, in open conflict with the imperialist order, came up against, as did those who conducted revolution in the name of socialism, the conflicting needs of catching-up (national construction) and the transformation of social relationships in favour of the popular classes. On this latter concern, the post-revolutionary regimes (or simply reconquered post-independence regimes) were certainly less radical than the communist powers, which is why I would describe these regimes, in Asia and Africa, as national/popular. They were also sometimes inspired by forms of organisation (single party, non-democratic dictatorship, state management of the economy) that had been developed during the experiences of actually existing socialism. They usually diluted their efficiency by their vague ideological choices and the compromise with the past that they accepted.

It was under these conditions that these regimes, like the critical avant-garde (historical communism in the countries concerned) were, in turn, invited to support the Soviet Union (and, more rarely, China) and benefit from its support. The constitution of this common front against the imperialist aggression of the United States and its European and Japanese partners was certainly beneficial for the peoples of Asia and Africa. It opened up a margin of autonomy, both for the initiatives of the governing classes of the countries concerned and for the actions of their popular classes. This is proved by what happened following the Soviet collapse.

The plutocratic oligarchies and the end of bourgeois civilisation

The logic of accumulation is that of the growing concentration and centralisation of capital. Contemporary capitalism is a capitalism dominated by a plutocratic oligarchy that is unprecedented in history, to which I have already drawn attention (Amin 2010, Chapter 4 and Amin 2008, p. 47 onwards).

The wheeler-dealers, the new dominant class in the peripheries

The centre/periphery contrast is not new; it accompanied the globalised capitalist expansion from the beginning, 500 years ago. Thus the local governing classes in the countries of peripheral capitalism, whether they were independent countries or even colonies, have always been subordinated governing classes, but nevertheless allied by the profits they obtained by being inserted into globalised capitalism.

These classes, most of them coming from those that previously dominated their societies before submitting to capitalism/imperialism, are very diverse. Their change, because of this integration/submission, is also considerable: former political mentors becoming large landowners, old aristocracies becoming leaders of the modernised state, and so on. The reconquest of independence often involved replacing these old subordinated classes (collaborators) with new governing classes – bureaucracies, state bourgeoisies, etc. They had greater legitimacy in the eyes of their peoples (at the beginning) because of their association with the national liberation movements.

But here again, in the peripheries dominated by the old imperialism (the forms preceding 1950) or by the new imperialism (that of the Bandung era until about 1980), the local governing classes benefited from a relative, visible stability. Successive generations of aristocrats and the new bourgeois for a long time, and then the new generation coming from the political forces that directed national liberation, shared value systems, moral and national. The men (and more rarely the women) who represented the governing classes, enjoyed various degrees of legitimacy.

3 HISTORICAL CAPITALISM – ACCUMULATION BY DISPOSSESSION

The upheavals brought about by the capitalism of the oligopolies in the new collective imperialist centre (the United States, Europe, Japan) have completely eradicated the power of all these old governing classes of the peripheries, replacing them with a new class that I call wheeler-dealers. This term has in fact spontaneously circulated in many countries of the South. A wheeler-dealer is a businessperson, not a creative entrepreneur. Businesspeople obtain their wealth from their relationships with existing power and the foreign masters of the system, whether it is representatives of the imperialist countries (the CIA (Central Intelligence Agency), in particular) or the oligopolies. Businesspeople operate as very well-paid intermediaries, who benefit from a veritable political rent, from which they draw the wealth that they accumulate. The wheeler-dealers do not belong to any system of moral or national values whatsoever. They are a caricature of their alter egos in the dominant centres, for they know nothing else but 'success', money and the covetousness that lies behind their alleged praise for the individual. There, again, mafia-like and criminal behaviour is never very far away.

It is true that phenomena of this kind are not completely new. The very nature of imperialist domination and the subordination of the local governing classes to it used to encourage the emergence of this kind of person in power. But, what is surely new is that this kind of person now dominates the whole scene of politics and wealth. The wheeler-dealers are the friends, the only friends of the dominant plutocracy at the world level. Their vulnerability lies in the fact that they have no legitimacy whatsoever in the eyes of their peoples, neither the legitimacy conferred by tradition nor that given by participation in national liberation.

Senile capitalism and the end of bourgeois civilisation

The characters of the new dominant classes described here are not coincidental; they correspond strictly to the requirements of contemporary capitalism and its functioning.

Bourgeois civilisation – like all civilisation – is not only reduced to the logic of the reproduction of the economic system. It integrates ideology and morality: praise for individual initiative, of course, but also honesty and respect for the law, if not solidarity with people, at least at the national level. This ensured a certain stability in social reproduction as a whole and it pervaded the world of the political representatives at its service.

This system of values is in the process of disappearing, making way for a system which has no values. There are many clear signs of this transformation: criminal US presidents, buffoons at the head of European states, insignificant autocrats in a number of countries in the South – who are not enlightened despots but just despots – ambitious obscurantists (the Taliban, the Christian and other sects, the pro-slavery Buddhists). They are all admirers of the American model, without any reservations. Lack of culture and vulgarity are characteristics of a growing majority of this world of those who dominate.

A dramatic evolution of this kind proclaims the end of a civilisation. It reproduces what we have already seen in the decadent epochs of history. A new world is being born. But not the (better) one which many of the naive social movements are calling for. They do, of course, see the extent of the destruction, but they do not understand the reasons. A world that is much worse than that of the bourgeois civilisation is being imposed.

For all these reasons, I consider that the contemporary capitalism of the oligopolies must be now described as senile – whatever its apparent immediate success – because it is a success that is sinking into a new barbarism. (I refer here to the concluding chapter, 'Revolution or decadence, thoughts on the transition from one mode of production to another', of my book *Class and Nation* (Amin 1981) written almost 30 years ago.)

The fragility of capitalist globalisation

Capitalism can be defined as the reversal of the relationship of dominance between the political body and the economic one. This reversal goes along with the new market alienation and the obscuring of social production, with the levying of the surplus that accompanies it (as Marx described).

This invention has produced positive effects, which in my view are indisputable and, therefore, irreversible. These are, among others, the liberation of the spirit of economic enterprise and overwhelming acceleration, through the rapid development

3 HISTORICAL CAPITALISM – ACCUMULATION BY DISPOSSESSION

of productive forces; the combination of conditions enabling the emergence of the social sciences (including economics), the formulations of which have been freed from morality and replaced by the search for objective causalities; and the emergence of modernity, formulated in terms of the emancipation of the human species, capable of making its own history and, with that, bringing together the conditions for modern democracy.

Capitalism is the first system that could become genuinely global. This was because of the power that it enabled to develop, far beyond that of the most advanced societies of the past. Thus the conquest of the entire planet became its objective. This power, which was already visible in the centuries of the mercantilist transition (1500–1800), appeared to be without limits from the Industrial Revolution onwards. Contrary to the naive vision of economists, capitalist globalisation involved the political (and military) intervention of the new imperial powers. It was through these unequal political relationships that markets were opened up and conquered, while the economic structures of the periphery, now dominated, adapted to the requirements of this form of expansion. The new polarisation, to an extent unprecedented in the history of mankind, was established by political means and not in any way by the victorious competition of the industries of the dominant centres. As a consequence, the countries of the periphery could reconquer their political independence without it putting an automatic end to their dominated status.

Polarisation is inherent in historical capitalism. Capitalism and imperialism are inseparable. Imperialist by nature, the world expansion of this historical system has shown that it was neither acceptable nor accepted by the majority of humanity – its victims – and that therefore it is considerably more fragile than believed by the economists, among others. The development of the crisis under way will certainly show this.

The status of a dominated country has never been accepted by the peoples concerned, apart from the new comprador classes that benefit from capitalist/imperialist globalisation. During the 20th century, this refusal turned into revolutions conducted under the flag of socialism or national liberation struggles, both victorious, which forced the imperialist powers to adjust to these unprecedented changes.

ENDING THE CRISIS OF CAPITALISM OR ENDING CAPITALISM?

The counteroffensive of capitalism/imperialism, which has been at work for some 30 years, has been made possible by the exhaustion of the alternative forms produced by the historic socialisms and nationalisms of the 20th century. This counteroffensive wraps itself up in the flag of globalisation. But, in fact, it cannot attain its aims without undertaking a new permanent war of reconquest. The project of contemporary globalisation is inseparable from the permanent military engagement of the dominant powers, the new Triad of collective imperialism.

Extrication from capitalist globalisation (what I call delinking) is a first condition for extrication from peripheral capitalist status (in vulgar terms, getting out of underdevelopment or of poverty). Extrication from capitalist/imperialist globalisation and extrication from capitalism cannot be dissociated. This equation creates problems and it is therefore crucial to know how it has or has not been taken into account.

The dominant thinking, which is essentially Eurocentric, is impervious to the arguments developed here. For these thinkers, there is no alternative to the western model. It has to be – and can be – imitated by others. That capitalism/imperialism has rendered impossible this development by imitation is beyond their capacity to understand.

Marxist thought is not Eurocentric by nature. Marx inaugurated the only way of modern thinking that was capable of ridding itself of the prejudices and the straitjacket of Eurocentrism. But the schools of historical Marxism were victims of its limitations. The drift from Marx took the form of the alignment of the European worker and socialist movement with a linear vision of history, which was not that of Marx himself. In this perspective, the socialist revolution could only occur when countries had become fully capitalist, as in the developed industrial world. Everywhere else the obligatory passage of a capitalist development through a bourgeois revolution was declared unavoidable. Historical Marxism to a large extent ignored the consequences of the inherent polarisation of historical globalised capitalism and hence the real nature of the challenge.

Polarisation delayed the necessary ripening of the socialist consciousness in the centre, whose peoples received benefits from the dominant position of their nations. In the peripheries it prevented

3 HISTORICAL CAPITALISM – ACCUMULATION BY DISPOSSESSION

the construction of new national capitalisms like those of the dominant centres, and hence it closed off the way to the bourgeois revolution. This created a double challenge for the alternative of popular revolution, that of accelerating the development of productive forces and simultaneously building social relationships that break with capitalism. There are therefore perspectives and strategies for the transition from world capitalism to world socialism that are different from those imagined by historical socialisms and Marxisms, and these have created new and unforeseen conditions for constructing the internationalism of the peoples.

Is lucidity possible in the transformative activities of societies?

The modernity of the Enlightenment, by declaring 'man' the author of his history, inaugurated a new chapter of history involving the possibility of lucidity.

Lucidity and alienation are the two opposite poles of the same dialectical contradiction. Lucidity is defined by the knowledge of need, and the power, based on this knowledge, to act freely and transform reality. Lucidity involves the emergence of a social science that makes it possible to know these objective necessities. In contrast, alienation is defined by the submission of human beings to forces seen as being exterior – supernatural – even if they are in fact the result of the human thinking and action that shape social reality.

Lucidity, which was absent from all premodern societies, European and others, thus understands that the passing from one stage of social evolution to another was not conceived and implemented by a social force that develops on its own (which one might describe as revolutionary). Rather, it develops by itself, through chaotic evolutions and is, therefore, associated with what one could describe as moments of decadence (from the old regime in decline). The passing from the slave society of the Roman Empire to the feudalism of the Middle Ages is a good example of this mode of transformation in which lucidity is lacking. Lack of lucidity is not the same as lack of intelligence. Our ancestors were no less intelligent than us; they were simply less equipped to control the necessary transformation, even when this control was only relative. Actors use tactics of intelligent actions. But they do not know where their choices will lead them; they do not pose the question of the results they will really be producing.

With modernity and the emergence of lucidity, the ways of transforming society underwent a Copernican revolution. The sages of the Enlightenment formulated, for the first time, a holistic and coherent project of transformation. This was to establish capitalism on the rubble of the Ancien Régime, a new society based on reason, itself a condition of emancipation. The project, which described what essentially became the bourgeois ideology, was in turn based on the separation of the regulations proposed for managing economic life (to be ordered on the principle of the new private ownership, the freedom of enterprise and to draw up contracts) and that of the model for managing political life (ordered by what was gradually to become democracy – respect for the diversity of opinions, removing the sacred from power and the formulation of human and citizens' rights). The two sides of the project were legitimate in terms of reason.

The lucid project of capitalist modernity to be constructed defined itself as establishing a transhistoric and definitive reason – the end of history, following non-reasonable prehistory. Auguste Comte, in his time, had a definitive vision which encapsulated the essential ideology of bourgeois modernity. But the victims of the new system of triumphant capitalism – the working classes – saw their project of transforming reality in a completely different perspective, that of overtaking capitalism and building socialism. By so doing they showed the relative character of bourgeois lucidity. From the idealistic formulations of utopian socialisms up to the one initiated by Marx – historical materialism – there is clearly visible progress in recognising the need to found the transformation project on the overtaking of capitalism and the building of socialism.

Associating the democratisation of society in all the dimensions of its economic and political management – and associating therefore this with social and human progress – definitively rejects the dissociation in the bourgeois formula of the Enlightenment and unmasks the market alienation that is peculiar to this formulation, in so doing giving the reason/emancipation association a new meaning, representing the advances in the communism project

3 HISTORICAL CAPITALISM – ACCUMULATION BY DISPOSSESSION

initiated by Marx. That this perspective, which in turn consigned capitalism to prehistory, had sometimes imagined the communist future as the authentic end of history is another story.

The fact remains that lucidity, however relative it may be, made it possible to invent the revolutionary path as a way of transforming society, replacing the decadence of the Ancien Régime and the crystallisation of the new through controlled chaos.

The revolutionary path was indeed the one that capitalism imposed, first in its early revolutions in the Netherlands and in England, then partly through the independence war of the English colonies of North America and finally, and above all, in the French Revolution. In its turn, the revolutionary path was imposed as a lucid way of transformation, as it proposed to open the way to socialist/communist construction. The revolution in question has often been seen as the great moment that makes it possible, once and for all, to give a rational/emancipatory response to the contradictions of a reality that has outrun its course (the Ancien Régime for the bourgeois revolutionaries, capitalism for the worker and socialist movements). One could compare the scope of these imaginary visions and replace, for the concept of the revolution (in the singular), that of revolutionary advances (in the plural) which take on different forms according to the conjunctures, but are always driven by an expression of objectives and means that aspire to lucidity.

At the present time we are being invited urgently to abandon what is described as the 'illusion of lucidity'. No doubt the reason is that the first wave of implementing projects for socialist construction wore out its capacities to successfully transform the societies concerned. Lucidity, which is always relative (sometimes the headiness of early success tends to make people forget this), is even brought into question as a very principle. However, the reasons for the collapse of the first wave of socialist projects should – with the benefit of hindsight – be very clear: historical Marxism, which inspired these projects, had underestimated – which is the least one can say – the polarising character of historical globalised capitalism. The second wave – to be created in the future – must draw the necessary lessons. The history of the formation of capitalism itself shows how it was a succession of waves that made it possible for the final victory to emerge: the Mediterranean wave of the Italian towns, which aborted, preceded by three centuries the wave of Atlantic mercantilism which prepared the success of the definitive form of European capitalism/imperialism and ensured its conquest of the world.

To renounce the principle of the will for lucidity means not opening up new avenues for the future, but closing them by a return to the obscurantism of the premodern epochs. This obscurantism is at the forefront of the scene at the present moment, in the trough between the collapse of the first wave of socialist advances and the emergence of the second wave, which is necessary and possible. This obscurantism takes on different forms, hard and soft. The hard versions take the form of a return to the apocalyptic hope, whose extreme and caricatured expression is found in the discourses of the sects, but its ravages are no less visible when it comes disguised behind the masks of so-called religious or ethnic fundamentalisms.

It is not a case of returning to the spirituality denied by the gross materialism of the consumerism of capitalist modernity but, in a more commonplace sense, it is the expression of people's powerlessness confronted by the challenges of ageing capitalism. The soft version contents itself with renouncing the idea of a coherent global project which necessarily poses the question of power, replacing it with the wonderful belief that individuals can change the world just by the miracle of their own behaviour. From the so-called autonomist movements to the philosophies – à la Negri – of the 'bobos' (see Translator's note) of our time, this soft mode of obscurantist renunciation of lucidity, by thus obliterating the reality of existing power (oligopolies, military interventions, etc), is now fashionable because its discourse is trumpeted by the media.

There is always a need for lucidity, even if it is, as always, relative. Abandoning it is like withdrawing into obscurantism and it can only lead to the horror of an uncontrolled transition towards another world which is still more barbaric than that of our senile globalised capitalism.

Lucidity involves supporting universalism, which is different from actually existing globalisation. The religious universalisms of ancient times (Christianity, Islam, Buddhism and others) which accompanied the formation of tributary empires should be considered as quite distinct from the necessary universalism, both modern ('man makes his own history') and socialist ('the progress of humanity must be based on cooperation and solidarity, and not on competition').

The renunciation of lucidity opens the way to the possibility of returning to the model of transformation through chaos and decadence. Senile capitalism can, in this way, inaugurate a new era of immense massacres, with the means available today. Nearly a century ago Rosa Luxemburg described the alternative: 'socialism or barbarism'. Today one could say: 'capitalism or civilisation?' Decadence and criminal chaos or lucidity and the renaissance of the socialist project?

References

Amin, Samir (1981) *Class and Nation*, New York, NYU Press

Amin, Samir (2003) *Obsolescent Capitalism: Contemporary Politics and Global Disorder*, London, Zed Books

Amin, Samir (2008) *The World We Wish to See: Revolutionary Objectives in the Twenty-First Century*, Monthly Review Press

Amin, Samir (2010) *From Capitalism to Civilization: Reconstructing the Socialist Perspective*, New Delhi, Tulika Books

Arrighi, Giovanni (2007) *Adam Smith in Beijing: Lineages of the 21st Century*, London, Verso

Bagchi, Amiya Kumar (2005) *Perilous Passage, Mankind and the Global Ascendancy of Capital*, Oxford, Oxford University Press

Losurdo, Domenico (2007) *Fuir l'Histoire*, Paris, Editions Delga

4

Revolutionary advances and catastrophic retreats

This chapter deals with the conjunction of imperialist external aggression and local reactionary forces, as well as the theoretical errors and insufficient practice by revolutionary forces. It poses the question: what democracy can serve the people?

There is no lack of examples of advances that have been followed by dramatic retreats. They fill the history of the 19th and 20th centuries. They constitute the history of the three great revolutions of the modern world (the French, Russian, Chinese) and of a few others (Haiti, Mexico). Retreats of the same kind may be emerging (Cuba, Vietnam). Less spectacular, but nevertheless real, advance marked the history of the peoples of Asia and Africa during the Bandung era (1955–80). But everywhere they have been followed by retreats that have gone as far as re-establishing the comprador power subordinated to imperialist dictatorship. I describe these retreats as the 'drama of the great revolutions'.

The socialist advances of the 20th century: Sovietism and Maoism

The Marxism of the Second International, which was worker-oriented and Eurocentric, shared with the dominant ideology of the period a linear vision of history, according to which all societies must pass through a capitalist stage of development (thus sowing the seeds of the idea that colonisation was historically positive) before being able to aspire to socialism. The idea was utterly foreign to them that the 'development' of some (the dominant centres) and the 'under-development' of others (the dominated peripheries) were inseparable, like two sides of the same coin, both inherently produced by the world expansion of capitalism.

4 REVOLUTIONARY ADVANCES AND CATASTROPHIC RETREATS

At first, Lenin stood some distance from the dominant theory of the Second International and successfully conducted the revolution in the 'weak link' (Russia), but always with the conviction that this would be followed by a wave of socialist revolutions in Europe. This hope was not fulfilled and Lenin then gave more importance to the transformation of rebellions into revolutions in the East. But it was left to the Chinese Communist Party and Mao to systematise this new perspective.

The Russian Revolution was conducted by a party that was well rooted in the working class and the radical intelligentsia. Its alliance with the peasantry (which the Socialist Revolutionary Party represented) – in military uniforms – came about naturally. The radical agrarian reform that resulted finally satisfied the old dream of the Russian peasants – to become owners. But this historical compromise carried within it the seeds of its limitations: the 'market', as always, created a growing differentiation within the peasantry (the phenomenon known as kulakisation).

Right from the start (or at least as from the 1930s) the Chinese revolution developed along different lines, guaranteeing a solid alliance with the poor and middle peasants. Furthermore, the national dimension – the war of resistance against the Japanese – also enabled the front directed by the communists to recruit a considerable number of people from the bourgeois classes who were disappointed by the weaknesses and betrayals of the Kuomintang. The Chinese revolution thus produced a new situation, different from that of post-revolutionary Russia. The radical peasant revolution got rid of the very idea of private ownership of agrarian land and replaced it by the guarantee for all peasants to have equal access to agrarian land. Up until now, this decisive advantage, which is not shared by any other country other than Vietnam, constitutes the major obstacle to a devastating expansion of agrarian capitalism. The question is now very frequently debated in China. The reader is referred to the chapter on China in my book *Beyond US Hegemony* (Amin 2006), and my article 'China, market socialism and US hegemony' (Amin 2005). But on the other hand, the rallying of many nationalist bourgeois to communist parties obviously exercised an ideological influence that encouraged the deviations of those described by Mao as partisans of the capitalist way ('capitalist roaders').

ENDING THE CRISIS OF CAPITALISM OR ENDING CAPITALISM?

The post-revolutionary regime in China not only had a number of substantial political, cultural, material and economic achievements to its credit (industrialisation of the country, radicalisation of its modern political culture, etc). Maoist China resolved the 'peasant problem' that had been at the heart of the drama of the empire's decline for two decisive centuries (1750–1950). For more on this subject, see my book *The Future of Maoism* (Amin 1983). Moreover, Maoist China achieved these results avoiding the most dramatic deviations of the Soviet Union: collectivisation was not imposed by murderous violence as was the case with Stalinism; opposition within the Chinese party did not end up in a reign of terror (Deng was put aside, then he returned).

The objective was pursued tenaciously of an unprecedented relative equality in the distribution of income between the peasants and the workers as well as between these classes and the governing circles – although of course with ups and downs. This was formalised by options of development strategy that contrasted with those of the Soviet Union (these choices were formulated in the 'ten great balances' at the beginning of the 1960s). It was these successes which later facilitated the successes of the development of post-Maoist China from 1980. There was also a contrast with India, which had not carried out a revolution; this is significant for understanding not only the different courses taken during the period 1950–80, but also the prospects for their probable (and/or possible) different futures. These successes explain why post-Maoist China, while now situating its developments within the new capitalist globalisation (through the policy of 'opening'), has not undergone destructive shocks such as those that followed the collapse of the USSR.

However, the success of Maoism did not 'definitively' (i.e. irreversibly) decide the question of the longer-term perspective for socialism. This was, first, because the development strategies of the 1950–80 period had exhausted its potential and the 'opening' (although controlled) became necessary (see *The Future of Maoism*, Part II, Chapter 2), which later involved the risk of reinforcing the tendencies to evolve towards capitalism. But it was also because the system of Maoist China combined contradictory tendencies on the reinforcement of socialist options or their weakening. Mao, conscious of this contradiction, tried to bend things in favour of

4 REVOLUTIONARY ADVANCES AND CATASTROPHIC RETREATS

socialism through the Cultural Revolution (from 1966 to 1974) and 'Fire on headquarters' (a reference to headquarters of the Central Committee of the Party, which represented the bourgeois aspirations of the political class to positions of power). Mao thought that if he succeeded in this correction of the course of the revolution, he could get the support of the youth (which, among others, largely inspired the European uprisings of 1968 – see the Godard film, *La Chinoise*). The outcome of these events showed what an error of judgement this was. Once the page of the Cultural Revolution was turned, the partisans of the capitalist path became confident enough to move on to the offensive.

The conflict between the socialist path, which is long and difficult, and the capitalist option, which is being implemented, is certainly not 'definitively resolved'. As elsewhere in the world, this combat, which opposes the pursuit of capitalist expansion to the socialist perspective, constitutes the real conflict of the civilisation of our time. But in this combat, the Chinese people have some great advantages, which are the inheritance of the revolution and of Maoism. These advantages function in various fields of social life: they are forcefully shown, for example, in the defence by the peasantry of the state ownership of agrarian land and the guarantee that everyone has access to it. Maoism contributed decisively in taking the exact measure of the issues and the challenge posed by the expansion of globalised capitalism/imperialism. Maoism makes it possible, in analysing this challenge, to focus on the contrast between the centres and peripheries that is inherent in the expansion of actually existing (see Translator's note) capitalism, imperialist and polarising by nature, and to draw all the lessons involved for the struggle for socialism, both in the dominant centres and in the dominated peripheries.

These conclusions were summed up in the beautiful, very Chinese formula: 'the states want independence, the nations, liberation and the peoples, revolution'. The states – that is, the governing classes (in all countries, when they are not lackeys and transmission belts for foreign interests) – are engaged in broadening the space that enables them to manoeuvre in the (capitalist) world system. They are also concerned to raise the position of the 'passive' actors (obliged to submit to unilateral adjustment to the requirements of dominant imperialism) to becoming 'active' actors (who participate in shaping the world order). The nations – that is, the historical blocs of classes that are potentially progressive – desire liberation, that is, 'development' and 'modernisation'. The peoples – that is, the dominated and exploited popular classes (see Translator's note) – aspire to socialism. This formula makes it possible to understand the real world in all its complexity and, on this basis, to formulate strategies of effective action. It has the perspective of a long – a very long – transition of capitalism to world socialism and thus breaks with the concept of the 'short transition' of the Third International.

Flood tide and ebb flow of the Bandung project (1955–80)

The second half of the 20th century saw unprecedented transformations in all the societies of the world. But it was in Asia and Africa, as they came out of the colonial night, that these transformations were the deepest, forced as these societies were to question the different degrees of capitalist logic. The page of 1492 was turned over, and the globalisation of the future was not the one that had been inaugurated five hundred years previously, dominated by western imperialism.

Nevertheless, after the flood tide of the Bandung era came the ebb flow. I have put forward some analyses of the progress accomplished and the reasons for later retreat, particularly of the most radical experiences in the two continents, in my recent book *L'Éveil du Sud* (Amin 2008), which I recommend to the reader.

I would suggest four recent cases for debate: Afghanistan, Iraq, Sudan and South Yemen. These are little and badly understood beyond the readers of Arabic and Farsi. Readers could complete the outlines given here with some supplementary writings about Afghanistan and Iraq.

These four societies are comparatively less homogenous than others from the religious or ethnic viewpoint. But that happens frequently in history, homogenisation often being a result of modernisation. This does not signify – far from it – that there is a 'natural animosity' between the different elements of a country, whether it is a question of Shiites or Sunnis, Arabs or Kurds (in Iraq), of people speaking Farsi or Turkish (in Afghanistan), of

4 REVOLUTIONARY ADVANCES AND CATASTROPHIC RETREATS

Muslims or non-Muslims (in Sudan) or of subjects of a feudal fragmentation (in South Yemen).

Nevertheless, this heterogeneity has, it seems, benefited the revolutionary response, because it accounts for the relative weakness of local powers, both the old 'independent' powers and those subordinated, through modernisation, to the protection of the imperial powers. It is the weakness of this power that it changes – in moments of crisis – into a break-up according to the lines that define this heterogeneity, while the revolutionary forces are able to take advantage of the general aspiration for unity of the people fighting against the existing powers.

These four countries are important from the viewpoint of the global interests of imperialism, which has difficulty in renouncing control over them: Afghanistan, once the frontier state with the Soviet Union and now with the central Asia that the imperialists are trying to build up against Russia; Iraq, whose sub-soil hoards some of the best oil reserves in the world; South Yemen, which commands the entrance to the Red Sea (the oil route); Sudan, control of which involves the control of Egypt (for the British of yesterday), rich in oil and uranium (today).

In these four countries, the minority 'modern' society, confronted by an apparently 'traditional' mass, has thus been particularly attracted by radical solutions, through a project of 'modernisation from above, supported from below', that had a socialist perspective.

Remarkable success of communist parties among the modernised minority

In Afghanistan, a monarchy which could be called feudal governed (barely) a collection of regions with vague borders, which were ruled over by their local masters. Its long attempt to resist the aggression of Britain, concerned to cut off the route of the Russians to the Indian Ocean and then of the Soviets in Turkistan, did not allow the country to acquire the homogeneity and strength to meet the challenge of social transformation. It is hardly surprising that the social and intellectual elites, who understood this failure, were naturally convinced, almost unanimously, that the (Soviet) socialist model was able to respond to this challenge.

In Iraq, the 'Sunni' monarchy imported by the British could not maintain itself except by renouncing its real independence. The Iraqi communist party was therefore able to win the hearts of the masses among the Kurds and the Shiite Arabs, winning minds among all the educated class, particularly among the students, of course, but also in large sectors of the new urban middle classes (professionals, army officers, etc). On the order of a monarchy that served the British, the communists opposed the reality of the millennial unity of Mesopotamia – the land between the Tigris and the Euphrates – in spite of its diversity.

In South Yemen, the British had reinforced a subordinated pseudo-feudal fragmentation, creating everything it needed. It divided the apparent local powers into a multitude of *mashiakhas* (the domains of the sheikhs or those that claimed to be such), of sultanates and emirates (reduced to a small town and three villages), reserving the port of Aden to direct colonial administration. The communist movement (unified under the name of the socialist party) had no difficulty in rallying all sectors of modern society (dockers, students, the urban middle classes) under the banner of 'abolishing the structures created by the British: unity, liberation, socialism'.

In Sudan, the communist party succeeded in winning over all the sectors of modern society in the country: the workers' unions (starting with the railway workers) which, although clearly a minority in the society, nevertheless represented an important force, not so much for itself but for the role it played for the people as a whole by its defence of the social rights of workers and the democratic rights of the popular classes in their own organisations; the peasants in the regions modernised by irrigation, which had been incorporated into capitalism in a more direct way; the women's organisations struggling against patriarchal oppression; the educated youths and students; the professions organised in unions by the party; and even a good number of officers in the army.

The communist parties of these four countries succeeded in making remarkable revolutionary advances: in Afghanistan and Yemen they conquered state power, in Iraq and Sudan they were not far from doing so

The communist party of Afghanistan (in fact two parties in

4 REVOLUTIONARY ADVANCES AND CATASTROPHIC RETREATS

one: Parcham – the Flag; Khalq – the People) did not come to power through a military *coup d'état* fabricated by Moscow (on the model of the CIA *coups d'état*), as unfortunately is widely believed in the West. It took over the declining power of the monarchy; the few communist officers who 'invaded' the palace did not set up a dictatorship, but opened the way for power to be exercised by the party. Moscow did not have much to do with it at the beginning; it had been quite happy with the monarchy's neutralist position in international politics. But one part of the communist party, confronted by the (military) aggression of the United States, which was foreseeable and inevitable (and indisputably this was a correct judgement), felt that Soviet support was necessary. The other part felt that this support would not strengthen the capacity of the country to successfully resist imperialism, but, on the contrary, risked complicating the task.

Afghanistan experienced the best moment of its contemporary history during the epoch of the so-called communist republic. It was a regime of modernising enlightened despotism, opening up education to both boys and girls and hostile to obscurantism, for which it had decisive support within society. The agrarian reform that it undertook was mainly a collection of measures aimed at reducing the tyrannical powers of the tribal chiefs. The support – at least tacit – of the peasant majorities guaranteed the probable success of this evolution, which started well. The propaganda transmitted by both the western media and political Islam presented this experience as one of 'communist and atheist totalitarianism', which was rejected by the Afghan people. In reality the regime, like that of Ataturk in his time, was far from unpopular.

The fact that its promoters, in their two major sections (Khalq and Parcham), described themselves as communists was not at all surprising. The model of the progress accomplished by the neighbouring peoples of Soviet Central Asia (in spite of all that could be said on this subject and the autocratic practices of the system), when compared with the permanent social disasters of the British imperial management of neighbouring countries such as India and Pakistan, had the effect – as in many other countries of the region – of encouraging patriots to understand the obstacle that imperialism constituted for all efforts at modernisation. The invitation that certain members of the party addressed to the Soviets to help them get rid of the others certainly weighed negatively in that it impeded the national-popular-modernist project.

In South Yemen, the party (officially 'socialist') consisted of five communist groups of different origins who realised that they had to merge (while keeping their own identities). The British had decided to hand over a false independence to some of their colonies (Aden and the Trucial States) and had developed a plan guaranteeing the 'pacific' transfer of power to feudal bodies (emirates and others) whose powers had been reinforced during the colonial period.

London's plan functioned without a hitch for the Gulf coast, producing the United Arab Emirates. The Socialist Party of South Yemen refused to play the game and succeeded in mobilising all the most active elements of society around its watchwords: real independence, abolition of the systems of political oppression claiming to be traditional and social justice. Its radicalism paid off: the forces that it mobilised entered Aden and then all the towns that functioned as the administrative centres of the country. They even short-circuited a rival current supported by Nasser and the regime of North Yemen. The advances that followed are equally incontestable, in particular the liberation of women, the rolling back of obscurantism and the opening up of the way to a modern and democratic interpretation of religion and a secular state. Its popularity was no less undisputed.

In Iraq, too, the fall of the monarchy in 1958 was not the result of a military *coup d'état*. The intervention of a group of officers (including communists, but also progressive nationalists) only crowned the struggles of imposing masses of people, in which the communist party played a decisive role (in cooperation with other Arab and Kurd organisations, which were progressive to different degrees). The Ba'ath party and the Muslim Brotherhood were remarkably absent in these struggles. Abdel Karim Kassem, who presided over the regime, was therefore supported by a political alliance that brought together the communist party, the progressive Kurds and the nationalists (independent of the Ba'ath party). The rivalry between the latter and the communist party was constant and lively, so much so that at a certain moment, supported by some officers who were communists or sympathisers, the communist party thought it could tilt the balance in its favour. Its failure to do so was due to a combination of interventions from

4 REVOLUTIONARY ADVANCES AND CATASTROPHIC RETREATS

the local reactionary forces (supported from outside), Nasserites and allied Ba'athists.

In Sudan, the strength of the communist party in modern civil society (workers, peasants from the Gezira, students, women, professionals and the army) was the reason why the dictatorship of General Aboud (supported by the British) was overturned, not by a military counter-coup, but by an enormous mass movement (the officers, in their turn, having refused to repress it). A long struggle followed, in which the traditional parties devoted to the colonial power (Ansar and Ashiqqa) were mobilised, supported almost unconditionally by the Muslim Brotherhood and the diplomats of Nasser's Egypt and Libya's Gaddafi. This reactionary, obscurantist and nationalist bloc (considered uncritically as anti-imperialist) was supported by western opinion against the most democratic forces of the country!

The victories of this reactionary bloc were always limited and fragile, and the communist party each time succeeded in getting back on its feet and making its opponents withdraw. The communist party did not try to instigate a military coup (which would have been fatal for it), as has been claimed. General Nimeiry was put in power by a military coup supported by a reactionary alliance: the Egyptian and Libyan diplomats, the Muslim Brotherhood, the United States and Great Britain. But not all the army officers were partisans of the coup. It was they (communist officers and sympathisers, progressive nationalists) who, without difficulty, isolated (and arrested) Nimeiry. After this success there was the possibility of a return to democratic civilian power, the place of the communist party having been reinforced. But a third reactionary military counter-coup (with, this time, the direct intervention of foreign powers, as well as Gaddafi) destroyed this democratic perspective. And ever since…

There were various causes for the failure of these four revolutionary advances. Some, of course, were specific to each case, but others were more or less common to all.

The first cause was the deliberate intention of the United States, Great Britain and their subaltern European allies to destroy these advances with the most extreme violence, including military intervention, implemented (in Afghanistan and later in Iraq) or seriously threatened.

As part of their strategy, the imperialists mobilised all possible and imaginable obscurantist forces, financing and giving them military equipment. In this they were helped by the Muslim Brotherhood. But it has to be said that they also benefited from the benevolent neutrality (and sometimes the complicity) of the nationalist populist regimes of Egypt and Libya.

The second cause stemmed from the very real difficulties in integrating certain parts of the 'middle classes' into the democratic bloc that supported the revolutionary advances. All efforts were made, very systematically, by – among others – the Muslim Brotherhood, supported by brutal actions of the power in place (prohibiting organisations, mass arrests and torture), to block the communist party's access to the popular masses.

As for the third cause, it was a result of the weaknesses in the theory of the various parties and of their analysis of a simplistic Marxism. The Russian Revolution had a strong echo in the East and the communist parties ranged themselves with no hesitation in the Marxism–Leninism camp, to which they remained verbally faithful until the collapse of 1990. This took them by surprise as they had never really posed questions about the nature of the system and its problems. Perestroika appeared to them to be a welcome new stage of development in triumphant socialism. They were ignorant of the profound crisis of Soviet society which was at the root of the problem. They considered the unfortunate choices of Gorbachev as simple mistakes, if not betrayal.

Convinced of the Marxist–Leninist nature of the Soviet Communist Party, these communist parties always rallied verbally to the positions defended by Soviet diplomacy, which was itself very attentive to developments in the strategic countries. I say 'verbally' because, in fact, these parties – or many of their cadres and leaders – in spite of everything, actually followed their own judgement and sidestepped the insistent interventions of Moscow. This was the case, for example, when Moscow insisted that the parties should dissolve and join with the nationalist parties in power (Nasserites and Ba'athists), which were described as being engaged in the 'non-capitalist way'.

The combination of all these elements, as well as others, explains the setbacks. In Afghanistan, the Soviet intervention – 'useless' is the kindest way of describing it – was capitalised on by

4 REVOLUTIONARY ADVANCES AND CATASTROPHIC RETREATS

the imperial powers, thus rallying the moderate nationalists of the Middle East. Without this intervention, it is possible that the progressive Afghan forces might have been able to hold in check the forces of Pakistan, the Taliban and all the obscurantists described in the western media as 'freedom fighters'.

In South Yemen, the communist power in effect committed suicide in 1991 by accepting unity with North Yemen. How to explain this incredible decision? Of course, Yemen constitutes one nation and there was a real desire among its people to get rid of the separation created by the British colonisation of its southern coast. But the relationship between North and South Yemen was not similar to that of West and East Germany, rather exactly the reverse. The ('backward') society and the political power of the North held no attraction for the South, even after the revolution had chased away the imam and replaced him with a populism that was inspired by the confused discourse of Gaddafi (whose power, in fact, does not have many progressive achievements to its credit). This is proved by the fact that, just after 'unity' had been proclaimed, the people of the South revolted in rejection of it, considering themselves betrayed by the leaders of the party. Savage military repression was necessary to impose unity. This is only a partial explanation: some of the party leaders (but not all), desperate after the collapse of the Soviet Union, wanted to rally to the camp of those they thought would ultimately be victorious. Some of them were afraid (correctly so) of a ferocious economic blockade by the West, perhaps a military intervention on some pretext or other.

In Iraq, the power relations could not be reversed except by the bloody dictatorships of Abdelsalem Aref, and then of the Ba'ath, with the unconditional support of the Muslim Brotherhood, of the autocratic, pro-imperialist regimes of the Gulf and even of Nasserite Egypt. Was not Nasser the 'father' of Kuwait's independence, fabricated by the British in 1961 and then supported by Egypt? The way was then open to the regime of Saddam Hussein.

In Sudan, the defeat of the attempts to stop the counter-revolution of Nimeiry opened the way to a regime that combined the dictatorship of the military with that of the Islamists. But in spite of the brutality of this type of power, the modern sectors of the society constituted a resistance front (but henceforth more passive than active), ignored by the West's 'friends of democracy'. The interminable war in the South, the breaking up of the country (provinces in the east, Darfur in the west) are the price that the Sudanese people pay for this undoing of its revolutionary advances. The intervention, 'humanitarian' among others, of the western powers does not redeem them from their close association with the assassination of Sudanese democracy – not to speak of the direct economic interests that motivate these interventions (particularly in oil and uranium).

Conclusions should focus on 'democracy'

Democratisation is a process that cannot be reduced to a static and definitive formula as in the contemporary 'representative democracy' that is generally proposed (multi-party, elections, human rights). Democracy is about all aspects of social life and not exclusively the management of the political life of a country. It concerns all the relationships between individuals, within the family, in the workplace, as well as the relationships between these and the economic, administrative and political decision makers. These relationships are at the same time individual and collective (the class relations are mainly the result of the unequal power relations in contemporary societies). Democracy means associating rather than dissociating political democracy and social progress. It also involves the recognition and the definition of the rights of the individual, formulated in terms of legal rights, and the institutional guarantee of their being genuinely respected. Individual freedom and the liberation of human beings from all forms of oppression are inseparable from the exercise of power by the people. A society is not advanced if it does not integrate the rights of the individual with those of the workers' and peoples' collective organisations.

The dominant ideology associates 'democracy' with 'freedom of the markets' (that is, capitalism) and claims that they are inseparable: there is no democracy without markets, therefore democratic socialism is inconceivable. It is only an ideological formulation – in the vulgar (see Translator's note) and negative sense of the term – which is tautological, inferring that the concept of democracy is reduced to that of the truncated US model.

4 REVOLUTIONARY ADVANCES AND CATASTROPHIC RETREATS

History does not bear out this viewpoint. Advances in democracy have already comes about as a result of popular struggles and have always been in conflict, to different degrees, with the fundamental logic of capitalism. In fact, the history of actually existing capitalism as a world system shows that even that truncated form of democracy has been the exception rather than the rule. In the very centres of capitalism, the progress of representative democracy has always been the result of popular struggles, resisted as long as possible by the holders of power (the owners). At the world level of the capitalist system – the real unit of operations for capitalism – the association of (truncated) democracy with capitalism even more visibly has no real grounds. In the peripheries that are integrated into actual world capitalism, democracy has never – or hardly ever – been on the agenda of the possible, or even desirable, for the functioning of capitalist accumulation.

In these conditions, I would go as far as saying that the democratic advances in the centres, while they have indeed been the result of the struggles by the popular classes, have at least been greatly facilitated by the advantages their societies have in the world system. Marx expected positive effects from universal suffrage: the possibility of a peaceful transition to socialism. History has not confirmed his hopes, as universal suffrage has functioned in societies that have become gangrenous through nationalist/imperialist ideology and the real advantages associated with it (see Canfora 2006).

The popular movements and the peoples struggling for socialism and liberation from the imperialist yoke were at the origin of genuinely democratic breakthroughs, initiating a theory and a practice that associated democracy with social progress. This evolution – beyond capitalism, its ideology and its limited practice of representative and procedural democracy – began very early, from the French Revolution. It was expressed in a more mature and radical way in the later revolutions, in the Paris Commune, the Russian Revolution, the Chinese revolution and a few others (those of Mexico, Cuba and Vietnam).

The Russian Revolution proceeded to make the great reforms that conditioned a possible socialist and democratic evolution: agrarian reform, expropriation of the capitalists. The state deviations came later. But it was without doubt the Chinese revolution that posed the principles of a popular democracy (which has nothing to do with the 'popular democracies' of Eastern Europe), making real social and democratic advances that define a stage in the long transition to democratic socialism.

The abolition of the private property of land and the guarantee of equal access to it for everyone constitute a major advance. The implementation of communes, of the collective management of agricultural production, of small, associated industries and of public services (schools, clinics, etc) could serve as an effective institutional framework for a gradual democratisation of the management of all these aspects of social life.

The limits, inconsistencies and retreats from popular democracy in China have many causes, which have been well analysed by Lin Chun (2006). They include the objective contradictions that oppose the three necessary thrusts towards a transition project over a long period (national independence, the development of the productive forces, progress towards the values of equality and socialism), but also – and no less important – the absence of formal legal guarantees for the individual and the imprecise institutionalisation of powers. The Maoists' 'mass line' that invited the popular classes to put forward their own demands, gave them the means of doing it, and did not raise the party as a self-proclaimed avant-garde, which 'taught' the people the truth of which it had the monopoly, without having to 'learn' from the people: all this stems from the fundamental logic of a democratic project. This principle is the very opposite of the thesis that theory comes from outside the movement. The 'mass line' is not, however, a substitute for the institutionalisation of rights and of organisations.

The capitalism of the oligopolies is the enemy of democracy. 'The market decides everything, the parliament (where it exists), nothing.' People thus risk being attracted to the illusions of identity (para-ethnic and/or para-religious), which are in their very essence anti-democratic, and so they are imprisoned in an impasse.

In the countries that we have mentioned here, the communist parties, far from having been anti-democratic by nature ('totalitarian' as western propaganda always repeats), have on the contrary constituted the most democratic forces in their societies, despite the limitations of their practices (so-called democratic centralism, etc).

4 REVOLUTIONARY ADVANCES AND CATASTROPHIC RETREATS

Sudan is a tragic example of the contradiction between the practice of representative, multiparty, electoral democracy on the one hand and, on the other, the urgent need for an authentic democracy that serves social progress. Several times in the contemporary history of Sudan (before the setting up of the military/Islamic dictatorship) – a country that was committed to free elections – the revolution in progress (supported by the people) was challenged by a (correctly) elected parliament, which was dominated by the traditional parties, who were enemies of both democracy (when necessary) and of social progress (always).

So, what is the alternative? The enlightened despotism of the party, as in Afghanistan? Some will say that it is an oxymoron: despotism is always anti-democratic, the Enlightenment was always democratic. This is a dogmatic simplification which does not stand the test of the necessary, continuing invention of new forms (including institutional ones) that go well beyond the western formula of representative, electoral democracy.

So is a single party the alternative? Or a front of different forces that are genuinely autonomous (not conveyor belts) but concerned to participate in a real convergence in the strategy for a long transition? The parties of the four countries considered here never settled this question, either in the bureaucratic sense that is commonplace elsewhere (which is to their credit) or in the sense of a consistent formulation of the alternative. This weakness stems from their summary interpretation of Marxism.

Actors of the new advances

Are these useful reflections for the actors of the new advances (especially in Latin America)?

I think so. Because while in Latin America electoral democracy has, in favourable circumstances, made undeniable victories possible as well as the formation of governments decided to engage in a progressive social transformation, the past history I have discussed here shows that these very quickly end up in an impasse.

The analyses and the strategies for pursuing struggles that I propose here go beyond those that were formulated in the Bandung era, from 1955 onwards. At that time, the regimes emerged from the national liberation struggles of Asia and Africa.

They were legitimate and popular because of this and were generally of a 'populist' nature, which was recognised in the practices of the state (often confused with its charismatic hero) and the party (manufactured at the top in certain cases, never very democratic in its practice, even when it was the heir of the popular mobilisations associated with the liberation struggles) in their relations with 'the people' (a vague substitute for the alliance of the identified popular classes).

The ideology on which the legitimacy of power was based did not make reference to Marxism. It was cobbled together, associating a past largely reinvented and presented as essentially 'progressive' (because of the so-called democratic ways in which power was exercised in the old communities and because of religious interpretations of the same kind) with founding nationalist myths. This amalgamation was done with a pragmatism that was hardly concerned about the requirements of technological and administrative modernisation. The self-proclaimed socialism of the Bandung regimes was vague in the extreme and difficult to distinguish from the populist statism that redistributes and guarantees social justice. Should one not point out the existence of many of these characteristics in the recent advances of Latin America, which has not had the opportunity of knowing the Bandung experience and so risks reproducing its limitations?

I have developed quite another vision of the question of socialism and am careful not to reduce the 'construction of socialism' to achieving even the whole of a current, maximally possible programme. I describe such a programme as 'national, popular and democratic', one which opens the way (but not more) to the long, secular transition to socialism. I avoid the simple phrase of 'socialism of the 21st century' and favour, instead, 'progress along the long route of the transition to socialism'.

From Nepal to India: a contagion?

At the very moment when imperialist globalisation seemed to be triumphing, a small country in the heart of Asia started a genuine revolutionary process.

A liberation army that supported the generalised revolt of the peasantry reached the gates of the capital where, in turn,

4 REVOLUTIONARY ADVANCES AND CATASTROPHIC RETREATS

the population rose to chase away the royal government and welcomed as a liberator the Communist Party of Nepal (Maoist), which had proved the effectiveness of its revolutionary strategy. It is the most radical, victorious, revolutionary advance of our epoch and thus the most promising. For comparison, it would be as if the FARC of Colombia managed to mobilise all the peasantry of the country (actually impossible to imagine) and link their victory to a popular urban uprising, chasing Uribe from Bogotá (equally impossible to imagine), thus enabling FARC to direct the new revolutionary government!

This victory in Nepal has created the conditions for a first success, that of a national, popular and democratic revolution, described by the party itself as anti-feudal and anti-imperialist. In fact, the generalised urban revolt, which involved both popular and middle classes, forced all the political parties to proclaim themselves, in their turn, as 'revolutionary republicans'. They had never thought of doing so a few weeks before the victory of the Maoists, having opted for peaceful struggle and the reformist path, and invested their hopes in elections. The other communist party, the Unified Marxist–Leninist Communists (UMLC), had joined the camp of the reformists, denouncing the 'adventurism' of the Maoists.

The Communist Party of Nepal (Maoist) had deliberately decided to make a compromise agreement with the other parties (the Nepal Congress, the UMLC and others) in the belief that they had acquired a minimum of legitimacy by rallying to the revolution, which could not therefore be easily contested afterwards. The compromise agreement did not solve future problems – on the contrary, it showed how enormous they were.

The first challenge was the agrarian question. The peasant uprising was the result of the correct analysis of the agrarian question made by the Maoists and the strategic conclusions, equally correct, that they had drawn: the great majority of the peasants, those who had no land (often Dalits in certain regions of the country), or were over-exploited tenant/sharecroppers or owners of tiny plots, were able to organise themselves into a united front and moved on to armed struggle, the occupation of land (including giving access to Dalits, which was denied them by the caste system in India) and reducing the rents paid to landowners, etc.

The uprising had, for these reasons, gradually spread throughout the country and the popular army, organised by the Maoists, inflicted defeats on the state army. But it is also true that when the revolt in the capital opened its gates to the (Maoist) Communist Party, the popular army had not yet managed to overcome that of the state, which was strongly supported and equipped by the government in Delhi and the imperialist powers.

The line defended by the Maoists is one of a radical revolutionary agrarian reform, guaranteeing access to land (and the necessary means for living on it) to all the poor peasantry (the great majority), without, however, touching the property of the rich peasants.

The second challenge was the question of democracy: was it to be bourgeois or popular democracy?

In Nepalese society there are the defenders of the conventional formula of democracy, which is reduced to multipartyism, elections, the formal separation of powers (among others, the independence of the judiciary) and the proclamation of human and fundamental political rights. The Maoists saw that the fundamental rights on which this democracy was based put respect for private property at the top of the hierarchy of so-called human rights. Instead, the Maoists defended the priority of social rights without which no social progress was possible: the right to life, to food, to lodging, to work, to education and to health. Private property is not sacred; it is limited by the requirements of implementing social rights. In other words, some in Nepal defended the concept of democracy dissociated from questions of social progress (the bourgeois and dominant concept of 'democracy'), while others supported democracy associated with social progress.

The debate – in Nepal – was not confused. The Maoists said that they did not object to private property, be it peasant, artisanal or even capitalist, national or foreign. They were not, however, against nationalisation if the national interest demanded it (prohibiting foreign banks from imposing the integration of the country into globalised financial markets). They only challenged the feudal land ownership, whose beneficiaries had been the clients of successive kings, who were authorised to dispossess the peasant communities. Nor did they challenge personal rights and the independence of a judiciary responsible for guaranteeing them.

4 REVOLUTIONARY ADVANCES AND CATASTROPHIC RETREATS

They added to this programme an invitation to the Constituent Assembly to formulate not only the main principles of social rights, but also the institutional forms necessary to implement them. Popular democracy, as they defined it, was to be invented gradually, through the actions both of the popular classes organising themselves and by the state.

Evidently, there is no guarantee that protects the future from the risk of things getting out of control. This could be the power of the state becoming autocratic. Or it could, just as likely, be an opportunist alignment about what is immediately 'possible', in which the Maoists might rally to the moderate line of their rivals. But why condemn the Nepalese in advance when all these questions are the object of serious debates within the party and when the plurality of opinions is accepted?

These analyses and strategies for pursuing the struggles go beyond those that were formulated in the Bandung era. The Maoists of Nepal have developed a completely different vision of socialism. They do not reduce the construction of socialism to the carrying out of their current maximum programme (radical agrarian reform, a people's army, popular democracy). They describe it as a 'national, popular, democratic' programme, opening the way (but not more than that) to the long, secular transition to socialism. They do not use the expression 'socialism of the 21st century'.

The question of the economic independence of the country is also a serious challenge. Nepal is classed by the United Nations as one of the 'least developed countries'. The modern administration of the state and of social services and infrastructure works depend, for this reason, on foreign aid. The present government is aware, it seems, of the need to liberate itself from this extreme dependency. But it realises that this can only be done gradually. Food sovereignty in Nepal does not constitute a major problem, even though self-sufficiency in this field means food rations that are often deplorable. The organisation of more efficient and less costly marketing networks for the producer peasants and urban consumers is, however, a problem because the interests of the intermediaries are at stake. To organise small-scale production that is half artisanal and half industrial and which is capable of reducing dependency on imports requires considerable time and effort to produce appropriate results.

The Maoist discourse is about a model of inclusive development, one which benefits the popular classes directly and at each stage of its implementation, as opposed to the Indian model of growth that is associated with social exclusivity, which benefits only 20 per cent of the population and condemns the other 80 per cent to stagnation, if not to pauperisation. It shows an option based on principles which one can only support. However, how it is to be translated into an effective programme for implementation remains to be formulated.

Revolutionary Nepal comes up against the ferocious hostility of its main neighbour, India, whose governing classes fear its contagious effects. The endemic revolt of the Indian Naxalites could, by getting inspiration from the lessons of the victories in Nepal, seriously affect the stability of the modes of exploitation and oppression in the Indian subcontinent.

The hostility of India should not be underestimated. It is one of the reasons for the military cooperation between India and the United States. The Indian government is mobilising considerable political means and it also finances, among others, the constitution in Nepal of an 'alternative' Hindu policy, along the lines of the Indian BJP and similar to the political Islam of Pakistan and elsewhere, as well as the political Buddhism of the Dalai Lama and others. These reactionary projects are receiving support from the United States and other western powers, particularly Great Britain. A Nepalese political Hinduism could crystallise if the objectives – even modest – of the new Nepal take too long to materialise. External intervention could also mobilise the reactionary Nepalese and even foment secessionist movements. The enemy has various strings to its bow, including the use of external aid, which is always conditional even if not admitted as such, and the demagogic discourses about 'human rights' and democracy, nurtured by the non-governmental organisation networks.

The advances in Nepal could be a forerunner of what might develop on the Indian subcontinent. The outcome of the – violent – political and social struggles which will certainly take place in India during the 21st century will determine the shaping of future

4 REVOLUTIONARY ADVANCES AND CATASTROPHIC RETREATS

globalisation. No doubt the governing classes of the country will try to advance successfully within the system of capitalist globalisation. A large majority of western observers share this illusion, as they are incapable of realising the growing extent of the social contradictions that these efforts will entail. It is thus possible that India will become the arena for the 'great revolution' of the 21st century, rather like China was in the last century, and that the objective realities will force India, in turn, to initiate the necessary and possible passage beyond capitalism. In these circumstances the contagion of the Nepalese model would have positive implications at the global level.

References

It is difficult to provide references as they are almost all in the Arabic language, or Farsi for Afghanistan (and perhaps in Russian). As far as the Arab world is concerned I should like to cite two important collections:

- The collection of studies on the communist parties, over 1,800 pages, put together by Fayçal Darraj, for the Arab Centre of Socialist Studies (Damascus). These studies are scrupulously honest concerning the facts and documents cited (the interpretation is, as always, a question of debate).

- The collection of studies on the Egyptian communist party (some 15 volumes of memoirs, documents and analyses), put together and published in Cairo by the Arab and African Research Centre.

More accessible to English-speaking readers are the following:

Amin, Samir (1983) *The Future of Maoism*, Part II, Chapter 2, New York, Monthly Review Press
Amin, Samir (2005) 'China, market socialism and US hegemony', *Review* (Binghamton), vol. XXVIII, no. 3, pp. 259–79
Amin, Samir (2006) *Beyond US Hegemony*, London, Zed Books
Amin, Samir (2008) *L'Éveil du Sud, panorama de l'époque de Bandung (1955–1980)*, Paris, Le Temps des Cerises, particularly for the advances in Nasser's Egypt, Mali and some others
Amin, Samir (2009) 'Nepal, a promising revolutionary advance', *Monthly Review*, New York, February
Amin, Samir (2010) *From Capitalism to Civilization*, Delhi, Tulika Books, in particular for the developments of the drama of the great revolutions and the contribution of Maoism (pp. 29–36)
Canfora, Luciano (2006) *La Démocratie, histoire d'une idéologie*, Paris, Seuil

Lin, Chun (2006) *The Transformation of Chinese Socialism*, Durham, NC, Duke University Press

5

Peasant agriculture and modern family agriculture

This chapter tackles capitalist agriculture and agriculture practised where capitalism predominates. It looks particularly at the land tenure reform that is necessary in Asia and Africa.

The North: family agriculture integrated into dominant capitalism

Modern family agriculture, dominant in Western Europe and in the United States, has clearly shown its superiority compared with other forms of agricultural production.

Annual production per worker (the equivalent of 1,000 to 2,000 tonnes of cereal) has no equal and it has enabled a minimum proportion of the active population (about 5 per cent) to supply the whole country abundantly and even produce exportable surpluses. Modern family agriculture has also shown an exceptional capacity for absorbing innovations and much flexibility in adapting to demand.

This agriculture does not share that specific characteristic of capitalism: its main mode of labour organisation. In the factory, the number of workers enables an advanced division of labour, which is at the origin of the leap in productivity. In the agricultural family business, labour supply is reduced to one or two individuals (the farming couple), sometimes helped by one, two or three associates or permanent labourers, but also, in certain cases, a larger number of seasonal workers (particularly for the harvesting of fruit and vegetables). Generally speaking, there is not a definitively fixed division of labour, the tasks being polyvalent and variable. In this sense, family agriculture is not capitalist. However, this modern family agriculture constitutes an inseparable part of the capitalist economy, into which it is totally integrated.

In this family agricultural business, its self-consumption no longer counts. It depends entirely for its economic legitimacy on its production for the market. Thus the logic that commands the production options is no longer the same as that of the agricultural peasants of yesterday (analysed by Chayanov) or of today in Third World countries.

The efficiency of the agricultural family business is the consequence of its modern equipment. These businesses possess 90 per cent of the tractors and other agricultural equipment in use in the world. These machines are bought (often on credit) by the farmers and are therefore their property. In the logic of capitalism, the farmer is both a worker and a capitalist and their income should correspond to the sum of the wages for their work and the profit from their ownership of the capital being used. But it is not so. The net income of farmers is comparable to the average wage earned in industry in the same country. State intervention and regulatory policies in Europe and the United States, where this form of agriculture dominates, have as their declared objective ensuring (through subsidies) the equality of 'peasant' and worker incomes. The profits from the capital used by farmers are therefore collected by segments of industrial and financial capital further up the food chain.

In the family agriculture of Europe and the United States, the land rent component, which in conventional economics is meant to constitute remuneration for the productivity of the land, does not figure in the remuneration of the farmer/owner, or the owner (when they are not the farmer). The French model of *anesthésie du propriétaire* (putting the owner to sleep) is very telling: in law the rights of the farmer are given priority over those of the owner. In the United States, where respect for property always has absolute priority, the same result is obtained by forcing, de facto, almost all family businesses to own the land that they farm. The rent from ownership thus disappears from the remuneration calculation of the farmers.

The efficiency of this family agriculture is also due to the fact that it farms (as owner or not) enough good land: neither too small, nor pointlessly large. The surface farmed corresponds, for each stage of the development of mechanised equipment, to what a farmer alone (or a small family unit) can work. It has gradually

5 PEASANT AND MODERN FAMILY AGRICULTURE

extended, as Marcel Mazoyer (Mazoyer and Roudard 1997) has demonstrated extremely well (by the facts) and illustrated (as an efficiency requirement).

Control over agricultural production is also exercised down the food chain by modern commerce (particularly the supermarkets).

In actual fact, therefore, the agricultural family unit, efficient as it is (and it is), is only a sub-contractor, caught in the pincers between, upstream, agro-business (which imposes selected seeds today, GMOs tomorrow), industry (which supplies the equipment and chemical products) and finance (which provides the necessary credits), and, downstream, the commercialisation of the supermarkets. The status of the farmer is more like that of the artisan (individual producer) who used to work in the 'putting out' system (the weaver dominated by the merchant who supplied him with the thread and sold the material produced).

It is true that this is not the only form of agriculture in the modern capitalist world. There are also large agribusiness enterprises, sometimes big owners who employ many waged labourers (when these estates are not leased out to tenant family farmers). This was generally the case with land in the colonies and still is the case in South Africa (this form of latifundia having been abolished by Zimbabwe's agrarian reform). There are various forms in Latin America, sometimes not very modernised and sometimes very modernised (that is, mechanised), as in the Southern Cone. But family agriculture remains dominant in Europe and the United States.

Actually existing (see Translator's note) socialism experimented with various forms of industrial agricultural production. The 'Marxism' underlying this option was that of Karl Kautsky who, at the end of the 19th century, had predicted not the modernisation of the agricultural family business (its equipment and its specialisation) but its disappearance altogether in favour of large production units, like factories, believed to benefit from the advantages of a thoroughgoing internal division of labour. This prediction did not materialise in Europe and the United States. But the myth was believed in the Soviet Union, in Eastern Europe (with some nuances), in China, in Vietnam (in the modalities specific to that country) and, at one time, in Cuba. Independently of the other reasons that led to the failure of these experiments (bureaucratic management, bad macroeconomic planning, reduction of responsibilities due to lack of democracy, etc), errors of judgement were made about the advantages of the division of labour and specialisation, which were extrapolated – without justification – from certain forms of industry and applied to other fields of production and social activity.

If the reasons for this failure are now recognised, this cannot be said for the forms of capitalist agriculture in Latin America and southern Africa mentioned above. And yet, their failure is also obvious, despite the profitability and the competitiveness of these modernised forms of latifundia. For this profitability is obtained through horrific ecological wastage (irreversible destruction of productive potential and of arable land), as well as social exploitation (miserable wages).

The South: peasant cultivators in peripheral capitalism

Peasant cultivators in the South constitute almost half of humanity – three billion human beings. The types of agriculture they practice vary: those who have 'benefited' from the Green Revolution (fertilisers, pesticides and selected seeds), although not very mechanised, have seen their production rise to between 10,000kg and 50,000kg per labourer, while for those whose practices are the same as before this revolution, production is only around 10 quintals per labourer. The ratio between the average production of a farmer in the North and that of peasant agriculture, which was 10 to 1 before 1940, is now 100 to 1. In other words, the rate of progress in agricultural productivity has largely outstripped that of other activities, bringing about a fivefold lowering of the real price.

Peasant agriculture in the countries of the South is also well and truly integrated into local and world capitalism. However, closer study immediately reveals both the convergences in and differences between the two types of 'family' economy.

There are huge differences, which are visible and undeniable: the importance of subsistence food in the peasant economies, the only means of survival for those rural populations; the low efficiency of this agriculture, not equipped with tractors or other materials and often divided into tiny plots; the poverty of the rural world (three-quarters of the victims of under-nourishment are rural); the growing incapacity of these systems to ensure food supplies for their towns; the sheer immensity of the problems because the peasant economy affects nearly half of humanity.

In spite of these differences, peasant agriculture is already integrated into the dominant global capitalist system. To the extent of its contribution to the market, peasant agriculture depends on bought inputs (at least of chemical products and selected seeds) and is the victim of the oligopolies that control the marketing of these products. For the regions that have 'benefited' from the Green Revolution (half of the peasantry of the South), the drain on the value of products by dominant capital is very great, both upstream and downstream. But, relatively speaking, the drain is also heavy for the other half of the peasantry of the South, given the weakness of its production.

Modernisation of agriculture by capitalism

Is the modernisation of the agriculture of the South by capitalism possible and desirable?

Let us use the hypothesis of a strategy for the development of agriculture that tries to reproduce systematically in the South the course of modern family agriculture in the North. One could easily imagine that if some 50 million more modern farms were given access to the large areas of land which would be necessary (taking it from the peasant economy and of course choosing the best soils) and if they had access to the capital markets, enabling them to equip themselves, they could produce the essential of what the creditworthy urban consumers still currently obtain from peasant agriculture. But what would happen to the billions of non-competitive peasant producers? They would be inexorably eliminated in a short period of time, a few decades. What would happen to these billions of human beings, most of them already the poorest of the poor, but who feed themselves, for better and for worse (and for a third of them, it is for worse)? Within 50 years, no industrial development, more or less competitive, even in a far-fetched hypothesis of a continual yearly growth of 7 per cent for three-quarters of humanity, could absorb even a third of this labour reserve. Capitalism, by its nature, cannot resolve the peasant question: the only prospects it can offer are a planet full of slums and billions of 'too many' human beings.

We have therefore reached the point when, to open up a new field for the expansion of capital (the modernisation of agricultural production), it is necessary to destroy – in human terms – entire societies. Fifty million new efficient producers (200 million human beings with their families) on the one hand, three billion excluded people on the other. The creative aspect of the operation would be only a drop of water in the ocean of destruction it requires. I thus conclude that capitalism has entered into its phase of declining senility: the logic of the system is no longer able to ensure the simple survival of humanity. Capitalism is becoming barbaric and leads directly to genocide. It is more than ever necessary to replace it with another development logic which is more rational.

So, what's to be done?

It is necessary to accept the need to maintain peasant agriculture for the foreseeable future in the 21st century. Not out of romantic nostalgia for the past, but simply because the solution to the problem is to overtake the logic that drives capitalism and to participate in the long, secular transition to world socialism. It is therefore necessary to work out policies to regulate the relationships between the 'market' and peasant agriculture. At the national and regional levels, these regulations, specific and adapted to local conditions, must protect national production, thus ensuring the indispensable food sovereignty of nations – in other words, the regulations must delink the internal prices from those of the so-called world market. A gradual increase in the productivity of peasant agriculture, which will doubtless be slow but continuous, would make it possible to control the exodus of rural populations to the towns. At the level of what is called the world market, the desirable regulations can probably be applied through inter-regional agreements that meet the requirements of a development that integrates people rather than excludes them.

5 PEASANT AND MODERN FAMILY AGRICULTURE

There is no alternative to food sovereignty

At the world level, food consumption is assured, through competition for 85 per cent of it, by local production. Nevertheless this production corresponds to very different levels of satisfaction of food needs: excellent for North America and western and central Europe, acceptable in China, mediocre for the rest of Asia and Latin America, disastrous for Africa. One can also see a strong correlation between food quality and the levels of industrialisation of the various regions: countries and regions that are more industrialised are able to feed their populations well from their own agricultural produce.

The United States and Europe have well understood the importance of food sovereignty and have successfully implemented it through systematic economic policies. But, apparently, what is good for them is not so for others! The World Bank, the OECD and the European Union try to impose an alternative, which is 'food security'. According to them, the Third World countries do not need food sovereignty and should rely on international trade to cover the deficit – however large – in their food requirements. This may seem easy for those countries which are large exporters of natural resources (oil, uranium, etc). For the others, the advice of the western powers is to specialise, as much as possible, in the production of agricultural commodities for export (cotton, tropical drinks and oils, agrofuels in the future). The defenders of food security (for others, not for themselves) do not consider the fact that this specialisation, which has been practised since colonisation, has not made it possible to improve the miserable food rations of the peoples concerned (especially the peasants). Nor is the correlation mentioned in the previous paragraph taken into account.

Thus the advice given to peasants who have not yet entered into the industrial era (as in Africa) is not to engage in 'insane' industrialisation projects. These are the very terms utilised by Sylvie Brunel (see *Alternatives Sud* 2008), who goes as far as attributing the failure of agricultural development in Africa to their governments taking this 'insane' option! It is precisely those countries that have taken this option (Korea, Taiwan, China) that have become 'emerging countries' as well as able to feed their population better (or less badly). And it is precisely those who have not done so (Africa) that are sunk in chronic malnutrition and famine. This would not appear to embarrass the defenders of the so-called principle of 'food security' (more accurately, 'food insecurity'). There is little doubt that, underneath this obstinacy over Africa committing itself to paths that the successes of Asia have inspired, there lies more than a touch of contempt (if not racism) towards the peoples concerned. It is regrettable that such nonsense is to be found in many western circles and organisations with good intentions (NGOs and even research centres).

Bruno Parmentier (2007) has clearly demonstrated the total failure of the 'food security' option. Governments who thought they could cover the needs of their poor urban populations through their exports (oil among others) have found themselves trapped by the food deficit that is growing at an alarming rate as a result of these policies. For the other countries – particularly the African ones – the situation is even more disastrous.

On top of this, the economic crisis initiated by the financial collapse of 2008 is further aggravating the situation – and will continue to do so.

It is sadly amusing to note how, at the very moment when the crisis underway illustrates the failure of the so-called food security policies, the partners of the OECD (such as the EU institutions) cling to them.

It is not that the governments of the Triad (United States, Europe, Japan) do not understand the problem. This would be to deny them the intelligence that they certainly possess. So can one dismiss the hypothesis that food insecurity is a consciously adopted objective? Has the food weapon not already been employed? There is, therefore, an extra reason for insisting that, without food sovereignty, no political sovereignty is possible.

But while there is no alternative to food sovereignty, its efficient implementation does in fact require commitment to the construction of a diversified economy and hence industrialisation.

5 PEASANT AND MODERN FAMILY AGRICULTURE

Land tenure reform vital for peasant societies

The main issue in the debate on the future of peasant agricultures is the rules governing the access to land.

The necessary reforms of the land tenure systems in Africa and Asia must be made from the perspective of a development that benefits the whole society, in particular the working and popular classes (see Translator's note), including, of course, the peasants. It must be oriented towards reducing inequalities and radically eliminating poverty. This development paradigm combines a mixed macro-economy (associating private enterprise and public planning) based on the double democratisation of the management of the market and of the state and its interventions, and the option to develop an agriculture based on peasant family cultivation.

Implementing this set of fundamental principles – the special ways and means of each country and phase of development will have to be worked out – constitutes in itself the construction of the alternative in its national dimensions. This must, of course, be accompanied by evolutions that can support it, at both regional and world levels, through the construction of an alternative globalisation, negotiated and no longer imposed unilaterally by dominant transnational capital, the collective imperialism of the Triad and the hegemony of the United States.

The regulations governing access to the use of agricultural land must be conceived through a perspective that integrates and does not exclude, which enables cultivators as a whole to have access to the land, a prior condition for the reproduction of a peasant society. This fundamental right is certainly not enough. It also has to be accompanied by policies that assist peasant family units to produce in conditions that help maintain the growth of national production (guaranteeing, in turn, the food sovereignty of the country) and a parallel improvement in the real income of all the peasants involved. A collection of macroeconomic proposals and appropriate policies for managing them has to be implemented, and negotiations concerning the organisation of international trade must be subordinated to them.

Access to land must be regulated by the status of its ownership. The terminology utilised in this field is often imprecise, because of a lack of conceptualisation. In English the words 'land tenure' and 'land system' are often used interchangeably.

First of all it is necessary to distinguish two families of land tenure systems: those that are based on the private ownership of land and those that are not.

Land tenure systems based on private ownership of land

In this case the owner disposes of, to use the terms of Roman law, the *usus* (right to develop), the *fructus* (ownership of the products of this exploitation) and the *abusus* (the right to transfer ownership). This right is absolute in that the owner can cultivate their land themselves, they can rent it out or they can even keep it out of cultivation. Ownership can be given or sold; it is part of a collection of assets deriving from the rights of inheritance.

This right is no doubt often less absolute than it appears. In all cases, usage is subordinated to laws governing public order (prohibiting land's illegal use for growing drug-producing crops, for example) and increasing numbers of regulations concerned with preserving the environment. In some countries that have carried out agrarian reform there is a fixed ceiling to the size of the property of an individual or a family. The rights of tenant farmers (length and guarantee of lease, the amount of land rent) limit the rights of the owners in different degrees, to the extent of giving the tenant farmer the greater benefit of protection by the state and its agricultural policies (as is the case for France). The freedom to choose crops is not always the rule. In Egypt, the state agricultural services have always imposed the size of the plots of land allocated to different crops as a function of their irrigation requirements.

This land tenure system is modern in the sense that it is the result of the constitution of actually existing capitalism, starting from Western Europe (first in England) and then moving to the colonies of European extraction in America. The modern land tenure system was set up through the destruction of the 'customary' systems of regulating access to the land in Europe itself. The statutes of feudal Europe were founded on the superimposing of rights on the same land: those of the peasant concerned and other members of the village community (serfs or freedmen), those of

5 PEASANT AND MODERN FAMILY AGRICULTURE

the feudal lord and those of the king. The assault on these rights took the form of the enclosures in England, imitated in various ways in all European countries during the 19th century. Marx very soon denounced this radical transformation that excluded most of the peasants from access to the use of land – and who were destined to become emigrant proletarians in the town or remain where they were as agricultural labourers (or sharecroppers) – and he classified these measures as primitive accumulation, dispossessing the producers of the land and the use of the means of production.

Using the terms of Roman law to describe the statute of modern bourgeois ownership implies that it dates from time immemorial, that is, that it dates back to the ownership of the land in the Roman Empire and, more precisely, to slave-labour land ownership. In actual fact because these particular forms of ownership disappeared in feudal Europe, it is impossible to talk of the continuity of a western concept of ownership (itself associated with individualism and the values that it represents).

The rhetoric of the capitalist discourse – the liberal ideology – has not only produced this myth of western continuity. It has produced another myth that is still more dangerous: that of an absolute and superior rationality of the management of an economy based on the private and exclusive ownership of the means of production, which include agricultural land. Conventional economics does in fact claim that the market, that is, the alienability of the ownership of capital and land, ensures the optimal (the most efficient) usage of these factors of production. According to this logic, therefore, land must be turned into a commodity like the others, which can be alienated at the price of the market to guarantee that the best use is made of it for the owner concerned and for the whole society. This is only a miserable piece of tautology, but it is what the whole discourse of the bourgeois economy is based on. This same rhetoric thinks it can legitimise the principle of ownership of land by the fact that it alone gives the cultivator who invests to improve the yields per hectare and the productivity of their work (and of those that they employ, if this is the case) the guarantee that they will not suddenly be dispossessed of the fruit of their labours and their savings.

This is not true at all, for other forms of regulations on the right of land use can produce the same results. Finally, this dominant discourse extends the conclusions that it believes to draw from the construction of western modernity, to propose them as the only rules necessary for the progress of all other peoples. Giving over the land everywhere to private ownership in the current sense of the term, such as that practised in the centres of capitalism, is to apply to the whole world the policy of the enclosures – in other words, dispossessing the peasants. This is not a new process: it was initiated and continued during the centuries preceding the world expansion of capitalism, particularly in the colonial systems. Today, the World Trade Organisation actually proposes to accelerate this process, although the ensuing destruction that this capitalist option involves is increasingly foreseeable and calculable. For this reason, the resistance of the peasants and the peoples involved can make it possible to build a real alternative that is genuinely human-oriented.

Land tenure systems not based on private ownership of land

This definition, being negative, cannot apply to a homogenous group. For in all human societies, access to land is regulated. But this is done either through customary communities, modern local authorities or the state or, more precisely and more often, by a collection of institutions and practices that involve individuals, local authorities and the state.

The customary management (expressed in terms of customary law or so-called customary law) has almost always excluded private ownership (in the modern sense) and always guaranteed access to the land to all the families (rather than individuals) concerned – that is, those who constitute a distinct village community and identify themselves as such. But it hardly gave equal access to the land. First, it usually excluded foreigners (very often what remained of the conquered people) and slaves (of various status); it also unequally distributed land according to membership of clans, lineage and castes, or status (chiefs, freedmen, etc). So it is inappropriate to indiscriminately praise these customary rights as – alas – is done by numerous ideologues of anti-imperialist nationalism. Progress will certainly require them to be questioned.

5 PEASANT AND MODERN FAMILY AGRICULTURE

Customary management has almost never been carried out by independent villages, which were in fact nearly always integrated into some sort of state, stable or shifting, solid or precarious, but seldom absent. The usage rights of communities and of the families that composed them have always been limited by those of the state that received tribute (which is the reason why I described the vast array of premodern production modes as tributary).

These complex kinds of customary management, which differ from one country and epoch to another, now only exist at best in extremely degraded forms, having been attacked by the dominating logic of globalised capitalism for at least two centuries (in Asia and Africa) and sometimes five centuries (in Latin America). The example of India is probably the most striking in this regard. Before the British colonisation, access to land was administered by the village communities or, more exactly, their governing castes, excluding the 'inferior' castes – the Dalits – who were treated as a kind of collective slave class, similar to the helots of Sparta. These communities, in turn, were controlled and exploited by the imperial Mogul state and its vassals (rajas and other kings), who levied the taxes. The British raised the status of the zamindars (whose responsibility it was to actually collect the taxes) to becoming 'owners', so that they constituted a kind of allied, large land-owning class, regardless of tradition. On the other hand, they maintained the tradition when it suited them, for example excluding the Dalits from access to land! Independent India did not challenge this heavy colonial inheritance, which is the cause of the unbelievable destitution of most of the peasantry and thus of its urban population (see 'India, a great power?' in Amin 2006).

The solution to these problems and the building up of a viable peasant economy of the majority thus requires agrarian reform, in the strict sense of the term. The European colonisation in South East Asia and that of the United States in the Philippines have had similar consequences. The regimes of the 'enlightened' despots of the East (the Ottoman Empire, the Egypt of Mohamed Ali, the Shahs of Iran) also mostly supported private ownership in the modern sense of the term for the benefit of a new class (incorrectly described as 'feudal' by the main currents of historical Marxism), recruited from the senior agents of their power systems.

As a result, the private ownership of land is now applicable to most agricultural land – particularly the most fertile ones – in all Asia, except for China, Vietnam and the former Soviet republics of Central Asia. There remain only the vestiges of para-customary systems, particularly in the poorest areas and those less attractive to prevailing capitalist agriculture. This structure is highly differentiated, juxtaposing large landowners (rural capitalists in my terminology), rich peasants, middle peasants and poor peasants without land. There is no peasant organisation or movement that transcends these acute class conflicts.

In Arab Africa (but not in Egypt), in South Africa, Zimbabwe and Kenya the colonial authorities granted their colonisers 'modern' private property, generally of a latifundia type. This inheritance has certainly been eliminated in Algeria, but there the peasantry had practically disappeared and been proletarianised or reduced to vagrancy by the extension of the colonial properties, while in Morocco and Tunisia the local bourgeoisie took over (which also partially happened in Kenya). In Zimbabwe the revolution under way has challenged the colonial heritage on behalf partly of new owners, who are more urban than rural, and partly on behalf of the 'communities of poor peasants'. South Africa, for the time being has not taken part in this movement. The strips of degenerated para-customary systems which remain in the 'poor' regions of Morocco and Berber Algeria, as in the Bantustans of South Africa, are suffering from the threat of private appropriation, encouraged by elements inside and outside the communities concerned.

In all these situations, the peasant struggles (and sometimes the organisations that support them) should be identified more precisely: do they constitute movements and represent claims by rich peasants who are in conflict with some state policies (and the influence of the dominant world system on them)? Or are they movements of poor and landless peasants? Could they both form an alliance against the dominant (so-called neoliberal) system, and on what conditions and to what extent? Can the claims – whether they are expressed or not – of the poor, landless peasants be forgotten?

In tropical Africa, the apparent persistence of these customary systems are certainly more visible. Because here the colonisation

5 PEASANT AND MODERN FAMILY AGRICULTURE

model took off in a different direction known as the *économie de traite*. This concept, which has no English translation, means that the management of access to land was left to the so-called customary authorities, who were nevertheless controlled by the colonial state (either through genuine traditional chiefs or false ones fabricated by the administration.). The objective of this control was to force the peasants to produce, beyond their own subsistence, a quota of specific export products (groundnuts, cotton, coffee, cacao). The maintenance of a land tenure system that did not recognise private property was convenient for the colonisers as land rent did not have to be taken into account in calculating the price of the products. This resulted in the degradation of soils, destroyed by expanding crops, sometimes definitively (as, for example the desertification of Senegal where groundnuts had been cultivated). Here, once again, capitalism demonstrates that the short-term rationality inherent in its dominant logic is largely responsible for ecological disasters. The juxtaposition of subsistence food crops and export crops also made it possible to pay peasants for their work at levels close to zero. For these reasons, to talk about the 'customary land tenure system' is grossly misleading: it is a new regime that conserves only the appearance of tradition, often its least interesting aspects.

China and Vietnam provide a unique example of a system for managing access to the land which is neither based on private ownership, nor on custom, but on a new revolutionary right, unknown elsewhere, which is that of all the peasants (described as the inhabitants of a village) having equal access to land (and I stress the equal). This is the most beautiful acquisition of the Chinese and Vietnamese revolutions.

In China, and still more in Vietnam, which had a deeper colonisation experience, the old land tenure systems (those I have described as tributary) were already fairly eroded by dominant capitalism. The old governing classes of the imperial power system had taken over ownership of agricultural land almost as private property, and the new classes of rich peasants were created in the ensuing capitalist development. Mao Zedong was the first to describe an agrarian revolutionary strategy based on the mobilisation of most of the poor peasants, who were without land or other assets. The victory of this revolution made it possible to abolish the private ownership of land right from the beginning – replacing it with ownership by the state – as well as the organisation of new forms of equal access to land for all peasants. True, this procedure has passed through several successive stages, including the Soviet-inspired model based on production cooperatives. The limits of their achievements led both countries to return to the idea of family peasant units. Are they viable? Can they produce a continual improvement in production without freeing up too much rural labour? On what conditions? What kinds of support are required from the state? What forms of political management can meet this challenge?

Ideally, the model involves the double affirmation of the rights of the state (the only owner) and of the usufructuaries (the peasant family). The state guarantees the equal division of the village lands among all the families and it prohibits all other usage other than family cultivation, for example the renting of land. It guarantees that the result of investments made by the usufructuaries are given back to them immediately through their right of ownership of all the produce of their land, which is marketed freely, although the state guarantees purchase at a minimum price. In the longer term the children who remain on the land can inherit from the usufructuaries (those who definitively leave lose their right to the land, which reverts to land available for future redistribution). This is the case, of course, for fertile land, but also for small, even dwarf-sized plots, so that the system is only viable if there is vertical investment (the Green Revolution but with minimal mechanisation), which proves as effective in increasing production through rural activities as horizontal investment (extension of the holdings, supported by intensified mechanisation).

Has this ideal model ever been implemented? The period of Deng Xiaoping in China, for example, was surely close to it. Nevertheless, even if it has created a greater degree of equality within a village, it has never been able to avoid the inequalities between one community and another, which are created by the differences in the quality of the soils, the population density, proximity to urban markets. No other system of redistribution (even during the Soviet-era structures of cooperatives and state marketing monopolies) has managed to resolve this challenge.

What is certainly more serious is that the system itself is subject

5 PEASANT AND MODERN FAMILY AGRICULTURE

to internal and external pressures that undermine its aims and social impact. Access to credit and favourable conditions for the supply of inputs are the object of bargaining and interventions of all kinds, legal and illegal: equal access to the land is not the same as equal access to the best conditions for production. The increasing popularity of the market ideology promotes this erosion: the system tolerates tenant farming (if not re-legitimising it) and the hiring of wage labour. The discourse of the right – encouraged from the global North – repeats that it is necessary to give the peasants 'ownership' of the land and open up the market in agricultural land. It is very clear that those supporting this are the rich peasants (if not agro-business), who want to increase their holdings.

The management of this system of access to land for the peasants has been ensured until now by the state and the party together. It may well be that this is on account of the village councils that have been genuinely re-elected and because there is no other way to mobilise the opinion of the majority and reduce the intrigues of the minorities of profiteers who would eventually benefit from a more markedly capitalist development. The dictatorship of the party has shown that this issue has been largely solved through careerism and opportunism, if not corruption. The social struggles under way in the Chinese and Vietnamese countryside make their voices heard in these countries just as they do elsewhere in the world. But they remain very much on the defensive, that is attached to defending the heritage of the revolution: the equal right of everyone to land. Defence is necessary because this heritage is more threatened than it would appear, in spite of repeated affirmations by the two governments that the ownership of land by the state will never be abolished for the benefit of private ownership. But now this defence requires the recognition that the peasants, who are those concerned, have the right to organise to carry out this defence.

Not only one formula for peasant alternatives

Agrarian reform should be understood as the redistribution of private ownership when it is considered to be unequally distributed. It is a land tenure system that is based on the principle of ownership. This reform becomes necessary both to satisfy the demand (perfectly legitimate) from poor and landless peasants and to reduce the political and social power of the large landowners. But where it has been implemented, in Asia and Africa after the liberation from old forms of imperialist and colonial domination, it has been carried out by hegemonic, non-revolutionary social blocs that were not governed by the dominated and poor majority classes. The exceptions were in China and Vietnam where there had not been an agrarian reform in the strict sense of the term but, as I have said, private ownership of land was suppressed, the principle of state ownership was affirmed and equal access to the use of land by all peasants was put into operation. Elsewhere, real reforms only dispossessed the large landowners to the profit, finally, of the middle and even rich (long-term) peasants, ignoring the interests of the poor and landless. That was the case in Egypt and in other Arab countries. The reform underway in Zimbabwe risks ending up in the same way. In other situations, reform is always on the agenda of what should be done: in India, in South East Asia, in South Africa and in Kenya.

The progress generated by agrarian reform, even where the reform is an immediate and essential requirement, is nevertheless ambiguous in its more long-term implications. For it reinforces attachment to 'small property', which becomes an obstacle to the questioning of a land tenure system based on private ownership.

Russia's history illustrates this drama. The developments that followed the abolition of serfdom in 1861 were accelerated by the revolution of 1905 because Stolypin's policies had already produced a 'claim for ownership'. This was (finally) fulfilled in the radical agrarian reform after the 1917 revolution. And, as we know, the new small owners did not enthusiastically renounce their rights for the benefit of the unfortunate cooperatives, which were dreamt up in the 1930s. Another path to development, based on the peasant family economy of the generalised small owners, would have been possible, but it was not attempted.

And what about the regions (other than China and Vietnam) where, in fact, the land tenure system had not (yet) been based on private property? This was of course the case with tropical Africa.

Here we find the old debate. Towards the end of the 19th century Marx, in his correspondence with the Russian Narodniks (Vera Zasulich, among others), dared to say that the absence of

5 PEASANT AND MODERN FAMILY AGRICULTURE

private ownership could constitute an advantage for the socialist revolution. It would enable a leap forward towards a regime for managing access to land other than the one governed by private ownership. But he did not specify what forms this new regime should take, the adjective 'collective', correct as it was, being insufficient. Twenty years later, Lenin believed this possibility no longer existed, having been eliminated by the penetration of capitalism and the spirit of private ownership that accompanied it. Was this a correct assessment? I cannot say, as I do not know enough about Russia. However, Lenin was hardly able to give decisive importance to this question, having accepted the viewpoint expressed by Kautsky (1899) in *On the Agrarian Question*.

Kautsky made generalisations about the extent of the model in modern European capitalism and believed that the peasantry was destined to disappear because of the capitalist expansion itself. In other words, capitalism would be able to resolve the agrarian question. While this was true (for 80 per cent) of the other capitalist countries (the Triad: 20 per cent of the world population), it is not the case for the rest of the world (80 per cent of its population). History has shown that not only has capitalism not solved this question for the 80 per cent of the world population, but that, as it pursues capitalist expansion, it cannot resolve it (other than by genocide – what a marvellous solution!). It was necessary to await Mao Zedong and the communist parties of China and Vietnam for an adequate response to this challenge.

The question came up again in the 1960s, when Africa attained its independence. The national liberation movements of the continent, the states and the state parties which it had produced, received, to different degrees, the support of the peasant majorities of their peoples. Their natural tendency to populism was to imagine a specific (African) path to socialism. This could be described as very moderately radical in its relationships both with dominant capitalism and with the local classes associated with its expansion. Nevertheless it posed the question of reconstruction of peasant society in a humanist and universalist spirit. This spirit was often very critical of traditions that the foreign masters had in fact been trying to mobilise for their own profit.

All the African countries – or almost all – adopted the same principle, formulated as the pre-eminent ownership right of the state over all the land. I am not among those who consider this declaration to have been a mistake, nor that it was motivated by extreme statistim.

To grasp the extent of the challenge it is necessary to study the way in which the current system controls the peasantry and how it is integrated into the world capitalist system. This control is ensured by a complex system that calls upon custom, private (capitalist) ownership and the state – all at the same time. Custom (as we have just seen) has degenerated and only serves as decoration in the discourses of dictators appealing to what is known as authenticity, the fig leaf to cover their appetite for pillage and betrayal to imperialism. The tendency for private appropriation to expand has not met with any serious obstacle, apart from some resistance by the victims. In certain regions, which are more suitable for profitable cultivation (irrigated areas, market gardens), land is bought, sold and rented without any formal ownership titles.

The pre-eminent state ownership (of land), which I defend as a principle, itself promotes private appropriation. The state can thus give away the land necessary for installing a tourist area, a local or foreign agro-business enterprise or a state farm. The title deeds required for access to the areas to be developed are the object of a distribution process that is rarely transparent. In all cases, the peasant families that occupied the areas and are forced to clear off are the victims of practices that amount to an abuse of power. But to abolish the pre-eminent state ownership of land in order to transfer it to the occupiers is not in fact feasible (all the village territories would have to be registered) and if it were attempted it would enable the rural and urban notables to make off with the best bits of land.

The right response to the challenges of putting in place a land tenure system that is not based on private ownership (at least not dominated by it) should be to reform the state and actively involve it in setting up a management system for access to land that is modernised, efficient (economically) and democratic (to avoid, or at least to reduce, inequalities). Above all, the solution is not to return to custom, which is anyway impossible and which would only serve to increase inequalities and open up the way to unbridled capitalism.

5 PEASANT AND MODERN FAMILY AGRICULTURE

However, it cannot be said that African states have never tried to take the path recommended here.

In Mali, just after independence in September 1961, the Sudanese Union started on what was very inaccurately called 'collectivisation'. In fact, the cooperatives that were established were not production cooperatives; production remained the exclusive responsibility of the family farmers. The cooperatives constituted a form of modernised collective power, replacing the so-called custom which the colonial power used to support. The party that took over this new modern power was also clearly aware of the challenge and aimed to eliminate the customary forms of power – which were judged to be reactionary, if not feudal. It is true that this new peasant power, formally democratic (the leaders were elected), was only as democratic as the state and the party. However, it did exercise modern responsibilities, seeing that access to land was carried out without discrimination. It managed the credits, the distribution of the inputs (which were partially supplied by state trading) and the marketing of produce (also partially delivered for state commerce). Nepotism and extortion were certainly not eliminated in these procedures, but the only response to these abuses was the gradual democratisation of the state, not its withdrawal, which was later imposed by liberalism (through an extremely violent military dictatorship), for the benefit of the traders (the *dioulas*).

Other experiences, like those in the liberated areas of Guinea–Bissau (inspired by the theories advanced by Amilcar Cabral) and in Burkina Faso during the Sankara era, have also openly confronted these challenges and sometimes produced unquestionable advances. There are now efforts to obliterate them from people's minds. In Senegal, the establishment of elected rural authorities constitutes a response that I unhesitatingly defend in principle. Democracy is a practice whose apprenticeship never ends, no less in Europe than in Africa.

What the dominant discourse at the moment means by reform of the land tenure system is the exact opposite of what is required for the building of an authentic alternative based on a prosperous peasant economy. What this discourse, conveyed by the propaganda instruments of collective imperialism – the World Bank, many development institutions, but also a number of NGOs that are richly endowed – means by land reform is the acceleration of the privatisation of land, and nothing more. The aim is clear: to create the conditions that would enable some modern islands of agribusiness (foreign and local) to take over the land they require to expand. But the supplementary produce that these islands could supply (for export or for local effective demand) could never meet the needs for building a prosperous society for all, which would involve the development of the peasant family economy as a whole.

Defining the role of the state in land reform

I do not exclude complex and mixed formulas for managing the access to use of land, which can be specific for each country. Private ownership of land can be accepted – at least where it is established and considered legitimate. Land distribution can – or must – be reviewed where this is necessary, by agrarian reforms (for sub-Saharan Africa, South Africa, Zimbabwe and Kenya). I do not even necessarily exclude the opening up of opportunities – under control – for setting up agribusiness. But the essential question lies elsewhere: how to modernise peasant family production and to democratise its integration into the national economy and globalisation.

I have no ready-made solutions to propose in these fields. I shall just mention some of the great problems that this reform raises.

The question of democracy is indisputably the issue that needs to be tackled in responding to this challenge. It is a complex and difficult issue that cannot be reduced to the insipid discourse of good governance and electoral multipartyism. It has, of course, a genuine cultural aspect: democracy wants to abolish the customs that are hostile to it (prejudices about social hierarchies and, above all, the treatment of women). Democracy includes juridical and institutional aspects: the construction of systems of administrative, commercial and personal rights that are consistent with the aims of social construction and the setting up of adequate institutions (elected, for the most part). But above all, the progression of democracy will depend on the social power of its defenders. The organisation of peasant movements is, in this sense, absolutely irreplaceable. It is only to the extent that the peasantry

5 PEASANT AND MODERN FAMILY AGRICULTURE

can express itself that the advances towards what is called 'participatory democracy' (in contrast to reducing it to the problem of 'representative democracy') can have a clear path.

The relationship between men and women is no less important in the challenge of democracy. Those who speak of family cultivation (peasant) evidently refer to the family, which up until now and almost everywhere has structures that impose the submission of women and the over-exploitation of their labour. The democratic transformation will not take place if there are no organised movements of the women concerned.

Attention should be given to the question of migrations. Customary rights generally exclude foreigners (that is, all those who do not belong to the clans, lineages and families of which the original village community is constituted) from a right to the land, or there are conditions attached to their access. The migrations caused by colonial and post-colonial development have sometimes taken on dimensions that upset the ethnic 'homogeneity' of the regions concerned. The emigrants who come from outside the country (like the Burkinabe in Côte d'Ivoire), or who although formally citizens of the same country are of an 'ethnic' origin that is foreign to the regions where they settle (like the Hausa in the Plateau state of Nigeria), have had their rights to the land they have cultivated questioned by narrow-minded and chauvinistic political movements, who also benefit from foreign support. One of the most unavoidable conditions for real democratic advance is to dismiss ideological and political communitarianisms and firmly denounce the para-cultural discourse that underlies them.

All these analyses and proposals, which come from past developments, only concern the status of ownership and the rules of access to land. These questions indeed relate to a major issue in the debates about the future of agricultural and food production of peasant societies and of the individuals who constitute them, but they do not cover all dimensions of the challenge. Access to land cannot be a potential transformer of the society if the peasants who benefit are unable to get access to the indispensable means of production on favourable terms (credit, seeds, inputs, access to the markets). National policies, like the international negotiations that aim to define the framework in which the prices and incomes are determined, are another dimension of the peasant question.

ENDING THE CRISIS OF CAPITALISM OR ENDING CAPITALISM?

I refer the reader to the writings of Jacques Berthelot on these questions. He is the best and most critical analyst of the projects to integrate agricultural and food production into world markets.

I shall just mention two of the conclusions and most important proposals that we have reached.

First: it is not possible to accept that agricultural and food production, as well as land, should be treated as ordinary 'goods' and thus allow them to be integrated into the project of globalised liberalisation promoted by the dominant powers and transnationalised capital.

The World Trade Organisation agenda must just be rejected, pure and simple. Opinion in Asia and Africa must be convinced of this, and particularly of the need for food sovereignty, beginning with the peasant organisations but also all the other social and political forces that defend the interests of the popular classes and of the nation. All those who have not renounced a project for development that is worthy of the name must realise that the negotiations underway in the framework of the WTO agenda will only be catastrophic for the peoples of Asia and Africa. Capitalism has reached the stage where the pursuit of profit requires 'enclosure' policies at the world level, like the enclosures that took place in England in the first stage of its (modern) development. Now, however, the destruction of the peasant reserves of cheap labour at the world level will result in nothing less than the genocide of half of humanity.

Second: it is impossible to accept the behaviour of the main imperialist powers (the United States and Europe) that are associated with the assaults against the peoples of the South within the WTO. These powers, which try to unilaterally impose liberalisation proposals on the countries of the South, have freed themselves from the same restrictions by ways that can only be described as systematic trickery.

The Farm Bill of the United States and the agricultural policies of the European Union violate the very principles that the WTO intends to impose on other states. The 'partnership' projects proposed by the EU, following the Cotonou Convention of 2008, are nothing less than criminal to use the strong, but appropriate, expression of Jacques Berthelot.

These imperialist powers can and must be accused in the very

5 PEASANT AND MODERN FAMILY AGRICULTURE

courts of the WTO set up for this purpose. A group of countries from the South can do this – and they must.

The alternative consists of national policies to construct/reconstruct national funds for the stabilisation and support for production, completed by the establishment of common international funds for basic products, enabling an effective alternative reorganisation of the international markets of agricultural products. Jean-Pierre Boris (2005) has elaborated such proposals in detail.

The peasants of Asia and Africa organised themselves during the stage prior to the liberation struggles of their peoples. They found their place in the strong historical blocs that made it possible to win victory over the imperialism of the time. These blocs were sometimes revolutionary (China and Vietnam) and then had their main rural bases in the majority classes of middle peasants and poor, landless peasants. Elsewhere, they were led by the national bourgeoisie or sectors among the rich and middle peasants who aspired to become part of it, thus isolating the large landowners in some places and the customary chiefs who were in the pay of the colonisers.

That page of history having been turned, the challenge of the new collective imperialism of the Triad will only be removed if historical blocs are constituted in Asia and Africa. But these cannot be remakes of the preceding blocs. The challenge faced by the so-called alternative world movement and its constitutive components of social forums is to identify, in the new conditions, the nature of these blocs, their strategies and immediate and long-term objectives. This is a far more serious challenge than is realised by many of the movements committed to the struggles.

A complex and multidimensional challenge

Is the capitalist modernisation path as effective as the conventional economists claim?

Let us imagine that, through capitalist modernisation, we can double production (from an index of 100 to one of 200), but that this is obtained by the expulsion of 80 per cent of the surplus rural population (the index of the number of active cultivators falling from 100 to 20). The apparent gain, measured by the growth of production per active producer is considerable: it is multiplied by ten. But, if it is seen in terms of the rural population as a whole, it is only multiplied by two. Therefore it is necessary to distribute freely all this growth in production in order simply to keep alive the peasants who have been eliminated and cannot find alternative work in the towns. It was in these terms that Marx wrote about the pauperisation associated with the accumulation of capital.

The challenge, which is to base development on renewing peasant societies, has many dimensions. I will just call attention here to the pre-conditions for constructing the necessary and possible political alliances that will enable progress to be made towards solutions (in the interests of the worker peasants, of course) to all the problems that are posed. The pre-conditions would include access to the land and to the means to develop it properly, reasonable wages for peasant work, improvement of wages parallel to the productivity of this work, and appropriate regulation of the markets at the national, regional and world levels.

New peasant organisations exist in Asia and Africa and are visibly initiating and active in the struggles underway. Often, when political systems make it impossible for peasants to constitute formal organisations, the social struggles in the rural world take the form of movements with no apparent direction. These actions and programmes, where they exist, should be analysed more carefully. What peasant social forces do they represent and whose interests are they defending? The majority mass of the peasants? Or the minorities who aspire to participate in the expansion of dominant globalised capitalism? We should mistrust quick answers to these questions, which are complex and difficult. We should be careful not to condemn a number of organisations and movements on the pretext that they are not mobilising the peasant majorities on radical programmes. This would be to ignore the need to formulate broad alliances and strategies by stages. But we should also be careful not to support the discourse of the 'naive alternative world people', who often set the tone in the forums and fuel the illusion that the world is on the right path only because of the existence of the social movements. This is a discourse that belongs more to the many NGOs – with good intentions perhaps – than to the peasant and worker organisations.

5 PEASANT AND MODERN FAMILY AGRICULTURE

I myself am not so naive as to think that all the interests that these alliances represent can naturally converge. In all peasant societies there are the rich and the poor (who are often landless). The conditions of access to land result from different historical experiences which, in some cases, have rooted aspirations to ownership in peoples' minds, while in others they have instilled the desire to protect the access to land of the greatest number. The relationships of the peasantries to state power are also the result of different political paths, particularly as concerns the national liberation movements of Asia and Africa: populisms, peasant democracies, state anti-peasant autocracies show the diversity of peoples' heritages. The ways in which international markets are run favour some and penalise others. These divergences of interest are sometimes echoed in many of the peasant movements and often in the divergences of the political strategies adopted.

Bibliography

The analyses and proposals put forward in this study do not only concern Asia and Africa. The agrarian questions in Latin America and the Caribbean have their own particularities and specifics. Thus, in the Southern Cone of the continent (southern Brazil, Argentina, Uruguay and Chile), modernised *latifundismo*, which is mechanised and benefits from cheap labour, is a form of exploitation well adapted to the requirements of the liberal globalised capitalist system. It is more competitive even than the agriculture of the United States and Europe.

Alternatives Sud (2008) 'Etat des résistances dans le Sud, face à la crise alimentaire', vol. 15, no. 4
Amin, Samir (ed) (2005) *Les luttes paysannes et ouvières face aux défis du Xxe siècle*, Paris, Les Indes Savantes. Includes references to peasant struggles in China, India, Philippines, Sri Lanka, Egypt, Ethiopia, West Africa, South Africa and Zimbabwe.
Amin, Samir (2006) *Beyond US Hegemony*, London, Zed Books
Amin, Samir (2006) 'India, a great power?', in *Beyond US Hegemony*, London, Zed Books
Berthelot, Jacques (2006) 'L'agriculture, talon d'Achille de l'OMC', http://www.solidarite.asso.fr
Berthelot, Jacques (2006) 'Quels avenirs pour les sociétés paysannes de l'Afrique de l'Ouest?', http://www.solidarite.asso.fr
Boris, Jean-Pierre (2005) *Commerce inéquitable: le roman noir de matières premières*, Paris, Pluriel

Chayanov, Alexander (1924 [1966]) *On the Theory of Non-Capitalist Economic Systems* (English edition)

Kautsky, Karl (1899 [1987]) *On the Agrarian Question*, London, Zwan Publications

Mafeje, Archie (2003) *The Agrarian Question, Access to Land and Peasant Responses in Sub-Saharan Africa*, Geneva, UNRISD

Mamdani, Mahmood (1996) *Citizen and Subject: Contemporary Africa and the Legacy of Late Colonialism*, Princeton, NJ, Princeton University Press

Mazoyer, Marcel and Roudard, Laurence (1997) *Histoire des agricultures du monde*, Paris, Seuil

Moyo, Sam (in preparation) *Land in the Political Economy of African Development*

Parmentier, Bruno (2007) *Nourrir l'humanité*, Paris, La Découvert,

Shivji, Issa (2008) interview by Marc Wuyts in *Development and Change*, Institute for Social Studies, vol. 39, no. 3

6
Humanitarianism or the internationalism of the peoples?

The revolutionary socialist tradition has always proclaimed itself to be internationalist, at least in its intentions, its visions of humanity and its socialist future.

This tradition was started by the French Revolution which in its radical moments abolished slavery, something that the so-called American Revolution never even thought of doing. The slaves (of Santo Domingo) fought to win their freedom (it was not given to them): they were citizens.

The new tradition could declare itself for the Enlightenment and for humanism, even if the concept of the latter was still in fact limited to the cosmopolitanism of the enlightened classes.

The socialist movement, utopian and Marxist, drew an imaginary picture of future world socialism and thus identified the needs of the struggle to give it greater consistency. When the International Workers Association was founded Marx made fun of the proposal by certain people who advocated the formula 'all the world are brothers' (Marx said he was not the 'brother' of all men!). He accepted instead the watchword 'workers of the world unite!' and he went so far as to say 'the proletariat has no country', a phrase that has since been wrongly interpreted by many people.

In practice, the worker and socialist movement of the capitalist/imperialist centres has not always been consistent on this issue. It drifted (see Translator's note) towards social imperialism which had a linear and determinist reading of history: first capitalism (in which the peripheries, believed to be 'backward' on the road that must lead them to it, must 'catch up') and then on to socialism. This drift was largely a result of what I have analysed as 'imperialist rent'. On the contrary, considering the contrast between the centres and the peripheries, there should have been a call to return the nations of the dominated peripheries to their place in the fight against capitalism, which is inseparable from imperialism. Moreover, this drift to social imperialism accompanied rallying to the (imperialist) country, to the point of accepting the chauvinistic calls for an inter-imperialist war. Is this no longer the case for Europe? (It is not for the United States and Japan.) Has it been superseded by the new cosmopolitanism of the European Union? It is by no means evident.

The historical Marxism of the Third International – Marxism-Leninism – wanted to break with this trend and it formulated a famous distinction – also badly understood – between 'bourgeois cosmopolitanism' and 'proletarian internationalism'. This distinction is, however, based on an extremely important objective reality: the gradual formation of the plutocratic oligarchy of collective imperialism. Thus this formulation was in some ways before its time: cosmopolitanism, understood as the solidarity of national fragments of the globalised oligarchy, conscious of the need for their collective management of the world system, is now more visible than it could have been before (or even after) the Second World War.

The abandonment of Marxism (of historical Marxism and, before it, of Marx himself), after the waning of the first wave of struggles for the emancipation of workers and of peoples in the 20th century, ended not in an increased consciousness of the need of the dominated and exploited for internationalism, but a retreat to positions of charity and humanitarianism. The central plank of this change was humanitarianism and development assistance, which helped to efface the real challenge: how to disengage from capitalism and, for the peripheries, how to start this off, by getting rid of dependence, aid, humanitarian charity, by delinking from the imperialist world system.

The first essential question: what kind of development?

It is not difficult to agree that a discussion on aid makes no sense without the country benefiting from the aid having a clear vision and development strategy.

6 HUMANITARIANISM OR THE INTERNATIONALISM OF THE PEOPLES?

From the 1981 meeting of the G7 at Cancún, the western powers proclaimed through the voice of Ronald Reagan, supported by his European colleagues, that the powers of the G7 countries knew better than the countries of the South themselves what was best for the South to do. The Washington consensus and the policies of structural adjustment put this position (return to colonialism) into practice through policies that have, effectively, been implemented ever since. In spite of the current deep crisis which should certainly challenge the global vision of liberal globalisation, this challenge is not in fact happening.

'Development' cannot be reduced to its apparently major economic dimension – the growth of GNP and the expansion of markets (both exports and internal markets) – even when it takes into consideration its 'social' dimensions (degrees of inequality in the distribution of income, access to public services like education and health). 'Development' is an overall process that involves the definition of political objectives and how they are articulated: democratisation of society and emancipation of individuals, affirmation of the power and autonomy of the nation in the world system.

This observation is all the more important because there is general agreement on the failure of development, as also on the failure of aid, because the countries concerned see that their dependency only increases rather than diminishing as time goes by.

The debate on aid is confined in a straitjacket, whose design was defined in the Paris Declaration on Aid Effectiveness (2005), drawn up by the OECD to be endorsed by (or, rather, imposed on) the recipient countries. Right from the start, the procedure was illegitimate. If, as is claimed, there are two partners in aid which are in principle equal – the donor country and the recipient country – the design of the system should have been negotiated by both parties. This was absolutely not the case. The initiative was unilateral: it was the OECD alone that was responsible for the drawing up of the Paris Declaration. Just like the United Nations Millennium Declaration, which was drafted by the US State Department, to be read out by the Secretary-General of the United Nations at the General Assembly, the Paris Declaration did not commit the international community. Also, the non-western countries that are not on the list of potential recipients of aid, particularly those which are themselves donors, refused, very legitimately, to associate themselves with the 'donor club' proposed by the declaration. If the international community was to commit itself seriously, a commission that had this responsibility should have been constituted in the United Nations, associating all the 'partners' from the start on the basis of true equality. The procedure adopted was part of the political strategy of the countries of the Triad (United States, Europe, Japan) to downgrade the United Nations and substitute it by the G7 and its instruments, claiming to be the international community, which is of course an imposture.

The field of responsibilities of the rich countries is defined according to the omnipresent principles of liberal globalisation. Sometimes this is explicitly stated: promoting liberalisation, the opening of markets, becoming attractive to foreign private investment. Sometimes it is indirect: respecting the regulations of the WTO. From this viewpoint, the Paris Declaration is a step back compared with the practices of the first development decade (1960–1970) when the principle of the countries of the South being free to choose their economic and social policies was more recognised.

The unequal power relationship between donors and recipients was further reinforced by insistence on the harmonisation of donor policies, which reduced the margins of manoeuvre that the countries of the South benefited from during the development decades. Instead of 'partnership', this relationship should be described as 'reinforcement of control over the assisted countries by the collectivity of the Triad states'. 'Partnership' is not progress but rather a regression compared with what used to happen during the Bandung era (1955–1980). If the word 'partnership' was put forward, it was precisely because that was not what was wanted. As George Orwell said, diplomacy prefers to talk about peace while it prepares for war. It is more effective.

Furthermore, the Paris Declaration has reinforced the means of political control by the Triad by adding to the general economic conditionalities (subject to the requirements of liberal globalisation – now in such disarray!) a number of political conditionalities: respect for human rights, electoral and multiparty democracy, good governance. The fact that the democratisation of societies is a long, difficult process, resulting from social struggles and policies,

6 HUMANITARIANISM OR THE INTERNATIONALISM OF THE PEOPLES?

is ignored. It absolutely cannot be replaced by the sermons of the heralds of good causes – national, let alone foreign – and still less by diplomatic pressures. Besides, in this field, reality – that is, the application of double standards – really hits one in the face.

The declaration tries to attenuate the gravity of the consequences of the strategies it promotes (structural adjustment, globalised liberalisation) by a new discourse, that of poverty and plans to reduce it, to which aid must give priority.

The feeble rhetoric of the new humanitarian discourse

The dominant discourse now aims at reducing poverty (eliminating it for those who think radically), with the support of civil society and replacing by good governance what was considered to be bad governance.

The very term 'poverty' stems from a language which is as old as the hills, that of charity (of religious or some other origin). This language belongs to the past, not to the present – still less to the future. It predates the language developed by modern social thought, which tries to be scientific by discovering the mechanisms that generate a phenomenon that is observable and observed.

Nor is 'social justice' a scientific concept. It is vague, imprecise by nature, and the means for achieving it go no further than listing measures that are not integrated (and are incapable of being integrated) into a coherent strategy. The contrast with the language of revolutionary France and of Marx, who called for equality and emphasised its contradictory complementarity with liberty (itself associated with property) shows how our thinking has regressed with this discourse on social justice. The nonsense of the North American jurist John Rawls, the sermons of Amartya Sen (a Nobel prizewinner) and the 'practical' proposals of Joseph Stiglitz (the rebel of the World Bank) cannot save this miserable non-thinking.

The expression 'civil society', so frequently used these days, comes to us from the United States. This concept is linked to a strategy constructed on the basis of 'communities', private enterprises that are believed to be closer to the public (consumers rather than citizens) and therefore more effective. It defines the common goods (education, health) but what it does in fact is to open up spaces for the expansion of capital. It contrasts with the European conception of public services and a civil society that is understood as all the popular organisations (see Translator's note) defending rights.

Civil society, in practice, rarely includes organisations that are rooted in the tradition of popular struggle (such as trade unions, peasant organisations, and worker and sometimes peasant political parties). The fashionable discourse prefers the non-governmental organisations (NGOs). This option is part and parcel of another aspect of the dominant ideology that sees in the state the natural adversary of freedom. In the conditions of the real world this ideology is used to legitimise the 'jungle of business', as is illustrated by the ongoing financial crisis. In the real conditions of the Third World, the pet NGOs are often called – ironically and rightly – GONGs (governmental NGOs), or MONGs (NGOs operating like the Mafia) or TONGs (NGOs transmitting donor policies), etc.

Civil society is therefore the collection of neighbourhood assemblies, of communities (the concept cannot be separated from the communitarian ideology), of local interests (school, hospital, green spaces) which are themselves inseparable from ideologies that are split up, separated from one another (gender understood in its narrow sense, respect for nature, which is also made into an object that is separable from the others). Even if the defence of the demands of these assemblies that constitute the so-called civil society is often legitimate, the absence – whether deliberate or not – of any integration into a vision of the whole society implies support for the dogma of consensus. In other words, to the extent that these demands succeed, it will be seen that 'the more it changes, the more it is the same thing'!

It is true that in these NGOs sectors of society express their defence of interests or of particular causes that are frequently legitimate (democracy and human rights, the rights of women, respect for the environment, etc), but sometimes they are ambiguous. Often they aim to make up for the shortcomings of the state (in education and health, for example). They are interclass organisations by nature, able to mobilise the middle classes, but they are much less successful with the popular classes. In these conditions,

6 HUMANITARIANISM OR THE INTERNATIONALISM OF THE PEOPLES?

this civil society does not offer an adequate framework for overall alternative projects, by definition consistent and political, to take form. Civil society is thus imprisoned into an anti-political, anti-state situation, sometimes a way of legitimising non-action; the discourse on the multitude (in the sense used in Negri and Hardt (2000)) serves this function. It is also the object of manipulations and has served, among other things, as a battering ram against socialist or national populist regimes. The deficiencies of these regimes are thus denounced not by the left but by the right, with the intention quite simply of supporting the return to capitalism. The underlying ideology, which is that of American liberalism, is an invitation to abandon the positive inheritance of left-wing political culture (the Enlightenment, emancipation and equality, alternative socialism) to the domination of capital over labour.

The term 'governance' was invented as a substitute for 'power'. The opposing characteristics of the two – good versus bad governance – hark back to Manichaeism and moralism, in place of an analysis, as scientific as possible, of reality. Once again, this mode comes to us from the other side of the Atlantic, where religious sermons have often dominated political discourses.

The notion of good governance assumes that the deciders are fair, objective, impartial and, obviously, honest. For oriental readers, the list of adjectives produced by the abundant literature of the American propaganda services is an immediate reminder of the grievances of ancient times, presented by the loyal subjects to the despot, who was asked to be fair (not even enlightened!). The proposals for establishing good governance institutions are no better: an interminable list of criteria, products of a bureaucratic imagination suffering from verbal diarrhoea.

The visible underlying ideology is just concerned with erasing the real question: what social interests does the existing power, whatever it is, represent and defend? How can this power be transformed so that it gradually becomes the instrument of the majorities, particularly the victims of the system such as it is? The recipe of electoral multipartyism has shown its limits in this respect.

All together, civil society, good governance, social justice and the war on poverty constitute a perfectly functional ideology; what is essential – the real power of the capitalist oligarchy – is eliminated from debate.

Humanitarian interventions, development aid, geo-economy, geopolitics and geostrategy

The choice of recipients and forms of intervention as well as of the aid's immediate, apparent objectives cannot be separated from the real geopolitical objectives underlying them.

Sub-Saharan Africa is very well integrated into the global system and is in no way 'marginalised' as, unfortunately, people often say without thinking: foreign trade out of the region represents 45 per cent of its GNP, as against 30 per cent for Asia and Latin America, and 15 per cent for each of the three regions that constitute the Triad. Africa is therefore quantitatively 'more' and not 'less' 'integrated, but it is so in a different way.

The geo-economy of the region is based on two kinds of production which determine its structures and the definition of its place in the global system: tropical agricultural products for export such as coffee, cocoa, cotton, groundnuts, fruit, palm oil; and hydrocarbons and mined materials, such as copper, gold, rare metals, diamonds.

The former category represents the means of survival – apart from peasants' subsistence crops – which finance the grafting of the state onto the local economy and, through public expenditure, the reproduction of the middle classes. The term 'banana republic' corresponds, apart from its negative implications, to the place that the dominant powers give to the geo-economy of the region. These agricultural products are of interest more to the local governing classes than they are to the dominant economies.

On the other hand, what interests the latter above all are the natural resources of the continent. Today these are the hydrocarbons and the rare minerals. Tomorrow, they will be the reserves for developing agrofuels, the sun (when the transport of electricity from solar energy becomes possible, which will be within decades), water (when its export, direct or indirect, is feasible).

Niger is a textbook example of all this. This country receives aid that covers 50 per cent of its budget. This aid is 'indispensable' for its survival although it is perfectly ineffective: the country remains close to the bottom of the list of the poorest countries in the world. But Niger is the third largest exporter of uranium in the world. Situated between Algeria, Libya and Nigeria, it could be tempted, through nationalism, to recover control over this wealth. Areva,

6 HUMANITARIANISM OR THE INTERNATIONALISM OF THE PEOPLES?

the French firm that exploits the uranium mine, knows this very well. It is not difficult to believe that aid to Niger has no other objective than to maintain the country as a client state.

The race for rural territory to be converted to the expansion of agrofuels is well under way in Latin America. Africa, too, offers enormous possibilities in this field. Madagascar led the way and has already conceded large areas in the western part of the country. The implementation of the Congolese Rural Code (2008), inspired by Belgian aid and the Food and Agriculture Organisation, will no doubt enable agribusiness to take over agricultural land on a huge scale in order to 'valorise' it, just as the Mining Code formerly facilitated the pillage of the mineral resources of this former Belgian colony. The peasants, who have been rendered useless, are the victims: their increasing destitution will perhaps attract humanitarian aid in the future, as well as aid programmes 'to reduce poverty'! I once learnt that an old colonial dream for the Sahel in the 1970s was to expel all the populations (the 'useless' Sahelians) in order to install extensive Texan-type ranches of livestock for export.

We are now in a new phase of history in which conflicts about access to the natural resources of the planet are becoming more acute. The Triad means to reserve exclusive access to this 'useful' Africa (that of the reserves of natural resources) for itself and to prohibit access to the emerging countries whose needs in this field are great and will no doubt increase. The guarantee of exclusive access is obtained through political control and reducing African countries to client states.

Foreign aid thus performs important functions in maintaining countries as client states.

In a certain way, therefore, it could be said that the objective of aid is to corrupt the governing classes. Apart from the financial misappropriations (which are well known but the impression is given that the donors are in no way responsible), this political function is served by aid which, as it is now the major source for financing budgets, has become indispensable. It is therefore important that this aid is not reserved exclusively for the classes in power in the government: it must also go to the oppositions that may succeed them. This is where the role of the so-called civil society and certain NGOs comes in.

Aid, if it is to be really politically effective, must also contribute to maintaining the integration of the peasants in the global system, which feeds the other source of income for the state. Aid, therefore, also has to promote the modernisation of crops for export.

In addition, it must facilitate access to common services (education, health, housing) by the middle classes and by some of the popular classes (mainly in the urban areas). The political functioning of the client state depends on this to a considerable extent.

In the Bandung era and during the development decades Asia and Africa, on the whole, initiated countergeopolitical policies, drawn up by the countries of the South, which aimed at counteracting the geopolitical policies of the Triad. The conditions of the period – military bipolarity, global overall growth and increasing demand facilitating the exports of the South – favoured this counteroffensive, forcing the Triad to make concessions, minor or major, according to the circumstances. In particular, military bipolarity prevented the United States and its associates in the Triad from reinforcing the power of their geopolitics by a geostrategy based on the threat of permanent military intervention.

These days, the geopolitics of the Triad, at the service of its geoeconomy, are reinforced by its geostrategic arm. It is now understandable why the United Nations has to be marginalised and substituted, cynically, by the military arm of the Triad's geopolitics, NATO. It is also understandable why the discourse about the external security of the countries of the Triad has become so insistent. All this rhetoric about the war on terrorism and the rogue states, which is intended to legitimise the strategy of the Triad, thus takes on dimensions that have become all too familiar.

The shape of an alternative international solidarity

A sudden rupture in ongoing aid – bad as aid is – is not desirable. In fact, it would be a declaration of war aimed at destabilising the existing power order and perhaps even at destroying the state. This is the strategy that sanctions have implemented, and continue to implement, the economic blockades of Cuba and Zimbabwe being good examples.

6 HUMANITARIANISM OR THE INTERNATIONALISM OF THE PEOPLES?

The choice is not between aid, such as it is, or no aid. The battle must be to transform radically the concept of the functions of aid, for which the South Centre has developed the arguments (Tandon, 2008). Solidarity, and not humanitarianism, is a major intellectual battle which should not recognise any red line that cannot be crossed.

This is one of the battles to be had among those that propose the construction of another, better, world, another globalisation, an authentically polycentric world system that respects the free – and different – choice of states, nations and peoples of the planet. Let us leave to the World Bank and the arrogant technocrats of the North the monopoly of producing valid recipes to be imposed on everyone.

The moral argument that the North owes a debt to the South, legitimising the principle of aid – as long as it becomes solidarity – is not without value. But more convincing – because they can mobilise political means to support them – are the arguments about the organisation of solidarity between peoples confronted by the challenges of the future, in particular the consequences of climate change. The UN Framework Convention on Climate Change (UNFCCC) constitutes an acceptable point of departure for conceiving of finance from the rich countries (which are primarily responsible for the deterioration of the world environment) for programmes benefiting the peoples of the planet, especially the most vulnerable. But, precisely because this initiative started off within the United Nations, the western diplomats have been busy – it is the least that can be said – in hindering its development (one might call it sabotage).

The drawing up of a global view of aid cannot be delegated to the OECD, the World Bank or the European Union. This is the responsibility of the United Nations and of that body alone. It is true that this institution is, by definition, limited by the monopoly of states, assumed to be representing their people. (But the same is true for the organisations of the Triad.) It is good that a proposal has been made for a stronger, more direct presence of the people, alongside their states, and it is worth discussing how this could be organised. But their presence must aim at reinforcing the United Nations. This cannot be done by substituting NGO participation (which would be carefully selected) in the conferences conceived and administered by the North (and inevitably manipulated by the diplomats of the North).

I would also give importance to the initiative taken by the UN Economic and Social Council in 2005 to create a Development Cooperation Forum (DCF). This would lead to the creation of authentic partnerships based on the conception of a polycentric world. As can be imagined, the initiative was not well received by the diplomats of the Triad.

But it is necessary to go further and dare to cross the red line. It is not a question of reforming the World Bank, the WTO, the IMF. It is not enough to limit oneself to denouncing the dramatic consequences of their policies, those of yesterday and those of today. What needs to be done is to propose alternative institutions, to define their tasks in a positive way and to shape the institutional arrangements.

The debate on alternative aid based on solidarity should immediately get rid of certain chapters in the OECD Development Assistance Committee's official development assistance compilations which in reality are not about aid from the North to the South, but rather the reverse. Heading this list are the concessional loans, given at rates that are claimed to be inferior to those of the market. These are the means by which aggressive commercial policies implemented by the states of the Triad help the main beneficiaries, which are in fact the exporters of the North (rather like the practice of dumping). Debt reduction, presented almost as a charitable act (as is clear from the diplomatic jargon in which the decision was couched) certainly does not merit being included as aid.

The legitimate response to this question, and not only from the moral viewpoint, should lead to an audit of all the debts in question – private and public, on the side of the lender and on that of the borrower. The debts recognised as immoral (among others, because of their association with corrupt operations on one side or the other), illegitimate (poorly disguised political support, as for the South African apartheid regime), usurious (rates fixed unilaterally by the so-called markets, by the integral reimbursement of their capital – and well beyond it): all these debts must be annulled and the victims, the debtor countries, recompensed for having overpaid. A commission of the United Nations should be created to draw up an international law worthy of the name

6 HUMANITARIANISM OR THE INTERNATIONALISM OF THE PEOPLES?

which, in this field, has hardly been started. Naturally, the diplomacies of the Triad do not want to hear of any such proposals.

The option for an alternative aid is inseparable from the formulation of an alternative development. I cannot go into this in any detail here. However, it is perhaps useful to recall some important principles about development in order to give greater meaning to proposals about alternative aid.

These important principles should include at least the following:

1. The problems of the rural world and of agriculture must be placed at the centre of a strategy for another kind of development, based on keeping large numbers of the rural population in place (even if there will inevitably be a decline in the numbers, the process should not be accelerated).

   As equal access as possible to land and the means for developing it properly must be the orientation of this conception of peasant agriculture. Its major features should include priority for food sovereignty; industrialisation, without which the achievement of these objectives is impossible; and a radical questioning of the globalised liberalisation of production and international trade in agricultural and food products (see also Chapter 5).

   The option advocated by the dominant system, which was not questioned by the Paris Declaration, is in complete opposition to the principles put forward here. This declaration is based on financial profitability, short-term productivism (rapidly increasing production at the price of accelerating the expulsion of surplus peasants), all of which corresponds very well to the interests of the agribusiness transnationals and those of a new class of peasants included as associates, but it is not in the interests of the popular classes and the nation.

2. Development requires the building of diversified productive systems, starting with those already on the way to industrialisation.

   The vital industrial perspective does not definitively rule out calling on international capital. Complex and diverse forms of partnership, state/local private (where it exists)/foreign capital, are completely acceptable – indeed, no doubt inevitable. But this development must have a perspective

that rejects liberalism, which is in essence about creating attractive conditions for the transnationals as advocated by the WTO and the so-called aid agencies. Real partnership in strategic decision-making and control over the re-exported profits must accompany industrialisation strategies.
3. Diversification (including of industrialisation), which is fundamental, certainly requires building infrastructures where they do not exist in countries receiving aid that has become indispensable for their survival.

   This includes social infrastructure: there is no development without good education, from bottom to top, and without a population in good health. Such objectives for aid (financial and technical) could undeniably be positive and become solidarity. The eradication of endemic diseases such as Aids is an obvious example.
4. In turn, diversification and industrialisation require building up forms of adequate regional cooperation. Countries that are continents may well do without them. But those with an average population (around 50 million) can only start the process, knowing that they will soon reach thresholds that they cannot cross except through regional cooperation.

   It will be necessary to reinvent these forms of regional cooperation so that they are consistent with the development objectives outlined here. The regional common markets, which dominate the institutions in place (where they exist and function) are not consistent with such objectives as they have been conceived as building blocks for liberal globalisation (see Amin and Tchuigoua 2005).
5. The alternative development sketched here requires control over foreign economic relationships, including abandoning the free trade system, which is claimed to be regulated by the markets, and instead, replacing it with national and regional systems of controlled trade. Beyond the impossible reform of the International Monetary Fund, solutions to the challenge should envisage the setting up of regional monetary funds, linked to a new system of world monetary regulation, which the present crisis makes more than ever necessary. The reform (or mini-reform) of the IMF does not meet these needs.

6 HUMANITARIANISM OR THE INTERNATIONALISM OF THE PEOPLES?

More generally, control over foreign relations, which does not mean autarchy, should define the outline of what I have described as 'delinking', essential if a negotiated globalisation is to emerge.

Such development also requires, obviously, national control over natural resources.

This alternative development is based on the principle of giving priority to internal markets (national and regional) and, in this framework, to the markets that meet the expansion of the demand from the popular classes and not from the world market. It is what I call 'autocentric development'.

6. The principle of the international solidarity of peoples, which I defend, legitimises support for struggles for the democratisation of society, associated with social progress and efforts to undertake reflection that is radical and critical.

With this in mind, public aid, which is certainly desirable in itself, must support the reconstruction of the state and its capacity to fulfil its functions (public services in the fields of education, health, water and electricity supply, public transport, social housing and social security), challenges which can be met neither by the private sector, which reserves for itself only the profitable parts of these activities, nor by associations, even the well-intentioned.

7. There will always remain a case for intervention in the name of universal human solidarity, which is perfectly legitimate.

Help for the victims of natural calamities and for the refugees that unfortunately wars produce in large quantities, cannot wait. It would be criminal to refuse help on the pretext that nothing had been done to prevent the deterioration of situations that were at the origin of these catastrophes (particularly warfare). Help first, then afterwards we'll see. Nevertheless the danger exists of an unacceptable political exploitation of 'humanitarianism'. There is no lack of examples, one of the most recent and most terrible being Haiti, where the aid provided in response to the January 2010 earthquake has given the US army an opportunity to reoccupy the country. On the other hand, necessary immediate help does not exclude opening up an investigation into the causes of the catastrophe. An independent critical

reflection on these problems is necessary and there should be a commitment to the social struggle necessary to rectify deteriorating situations that goes beyond the immediate humanitarian intervention.
8. North–South cooperation is not exclusive. There was South–South cooperation during the Bandung era and it was effective in the conditions of that time. Support for the liberation movements in the Portuguese colonies, Zimbabwe and South Africa, which was given by the Non-Aligned Movement (the OAU of that period), China, the Soviet Union and Cuba, was important and sometimes decisive. Then, apart from Sweden and some other Scandinavian countries, there was no development cooperation from the countries of the Triad, which were subordinated to the diplomatic priorities of NATO (including Portugal) and support for apartheid.

Today there are ample opportunities for renewing this South–South cooperation. The South now has access to means that enable it to break the monopolies upon which the supremacy of the Triad was based. Certain countries of the South are now capable not only of assimilating the technologies that the North wants to protect for its own use (precisely because it has now become vulnerable), but also of developing them still further on their own. If they wish to put them at the service of a different development model, more appropriate for the needs of the countries of the South, this could open an important new field for South–South cooperation. The countries of the South could also give priority access to the natural resources that they can control to reinforce their own industrialisation and that of their partners in South–South cooperation.

Certain countries of the South have access to financial surpluses which, instead of being placed in the financial and monetary markets controlled by the Triad, now facing collapse, could break the monopoly of the North in this field and the blackmail of aid that goes with it.

The South can do without the North but the reverse is not true. But to achieve this, it is necessary that the peoples and the leaders of the South free themselves from their way of thinking that interiorises dependency and that they cease to believe that aid constitutes the condition for the development of their societies.

Bibliography

In the order in which they appear:

Amin, Samir (1973) *Neo-Colonialism in West Africa*, London, Penguin Books (includes references to Niger)

Tandon, Yash (2008) *Ending Aid Dependence*, Oxford and Geneva, Pambazuka Press and South Centre

Amin, Samir (2006) 'The Millennium Development Goals', *Monthly Review*, vol. 57, no. 10

Orwell, George (1949 [2008]) *Nineteen Eighty Four*, London, Penguin Books

Amin, Samir (2003) 'Africa in the world', in Lauer, Helen (ed.) *History and Philosophy of Science*, Ibadan, Hope Publications

Bednik, Anna (July 2008) 'Niger's mine war', *Le Monde Diplomatique*, (English edition)

Amin, Samir and Tchuigoua, Bernard Founou (2005) 'Les régionalisations, quelles régionalisations?' http://www.forumtiersmonde.net. Partially reproduced in Amin S. et al., *Afrique, exclusion programmée ou Renaissance?*, Maisonneuve et Larose, p. 129 onwards

Ndiaye, Abdourahmane (2008) 'Avenir des agricultures et des sociétés paysannes en Afrique de l'Ouest, Une lecture critique des travaux du Club du Sahel', October, http://tiny.cc/kb0tw, accessed 24 June 2010

Berthelot, Jacques 'OMC et Sud', http://www.solidarite.asso.fr

Berthelot, Jacques 'La question agricole', http://www.solidarite.asso.fr

Berthelot, Jacques (2008), 'Démêler le vrai du faux dans la flambée des prix agricoles mondiaux', 6 October, http://www.cadtm.org/Demeler-le-vrai-du-faux-dans-la, accessed 24 June 2010

Berthelot, Jacques 'Cinq bonnes raisons pour ne pas signer l'APE-AO'

Boris, Jean-Pierre (2005) *Commerce inéquitable: Le roman noir des matières premières*, Paris, Pluriel

Amin, Samir (2009) 'Aid for Development?' in Abbas, Hakima and Niyiragira, Yves (eds) *Aid to Africa: Redeemer or Coloniser?* Oxford, Pambazuka Press

Negri, Antonio and Hardt, Michael (2000) *Empire*, Harvard, Harvard University Press

Negri, Antonio and Hardt, Michael (2004) *Multitude: Guerre et démocratie à l'âge de l'Empire*, Paris, La Découverte

7

Being Marxist, being communist, being internationalist

I am a Marxist. And by that I mean that Marx is my point of departure. I am convinced that the criticism that Marx put on the agenda of thought and action – the criticism of capitalism, the criticism of its main representation (the political economy of capital), the criticism of politics and its discourses – all these constitute a central and essential theme for the struggles to achieve emancipation for the workers and for the peoples.

I am not a neo-Marxist. To be one is to confuse Marx and historical Marxism, which is not my case. The neo-Marxists want to break with historical Marxism and they think by doing so it is necessary 'to go beyond Marx'. In fact they are only against those I describe as 'paleo-Marxists', that is those who unconditionally support historical Marxism, particularly Marxism-Leninism, in its various versions.

To be Marxist, as I understand it, is to be neither 'Marxian' (those who find such and such a theory of Marx to be interesting, isolated from the work as a whole) nor 'Marxologue'. It necessarily means being a communist – because Marx does not dissociate theory from practice. It is not possible to follow the traces of Marx without engaging in the struggle for the emancipation of the workers and of peoples. To be communist means also being an internationalist. This is not only a requirement of human reasoning. It is impossible to change the world while forgetting about the immense majority of peoples who form part of it, those of the peripheries. Now the onus is on these peoples to take responsibility for their future. It is not the peoples of the rich imperialist centres who alone can change the world (for the better!). They wish to substitute charity, aid and humanitarianism for internationalism,

7 BEING MARXIST, BEING COMMUNIST, BEING INTERNATIONALIST

in the sense of solidarity in struggle. This only contributes to the consolidation of the world such as it is or, worse still, involves constructing apartheid on a world scale.

In the following text I try to make more explicit the conclusions at which I have now arrived concerning the criticism of capitalism and that of the struggles in which its victims are engaged. They are not 'definitive conclusions' – a term that is alien to my way of thinking (which here, I believe, joins that of Marx). A good number of the central theses that I present have their histories in the development of my work. From one formulation to the next, I have obviously benefited from new readings – and re-readings – but I have also tried to take into account the evolutions of capitalism and the struggles that have been taking place in the meantime. To make the text easier I have not made references to the development of the concepts and proposals as they evolved.

Political and social conflicts and their representation

I insist on reversing the relationship of politics and economics, by which I define capitalism.

This reversal – economics becoming dominant and substituting for politics – indicates a qualitative change in history. The social system of capitalism is not just a system of classes, like those that preceded it, only based on a more advanced level of development of productive forces. The bourgeoisie does not have a conflictual relationship with the proletariat like the aristocracy's relationship with the peasants. The relationship is not only one of exploitation (which it is in both cases), it is a qualitatively new one. I also stress the qualitative transformation of the dominant ideology (I prefer the term 'representation' – see below), which was metaphysical in the *anciens régimes* and economistic in capitalism.

Isabelle Garo's convincing book *Marx, Une Critique de la Philosophie* confirmed me in my reading of Marx, but this reading is not dominant in historical Marxisms.

The capitalist state is not only a class state, like the state of the Ancien Régime. It is also a state that is qualitatively new. Politics is not the pursuit of the exercise of power for the benefit of the dominant class, as it used to be. It is qualitatively different politics.

It is in this sense that my emphasis on the rupture that the invention of modernity represents is justified.

The relationship between the political conflicts (the state) and the class struggle (in the sphere of economic and social management) is peculiar to capitalism, different from the way it was before capitalism.

At the heart of this transformation lies the novelty introduced by modernity: the declaration that human beings, individually and collectively, make their own history and want to do so in the way they choose, rather than as used to be done by God, ancestors and customs. This transformation makes democracy necessary and possible. In itself this is a new dimension of social life, which has only distant relationships with Athenian democracy or with all the forms of consultation and organised debates about the decisions to be taken in the old societies. Neither the Islamic *shura*, nor the African palavers round a tree, nor the Indian village councils are comparable with modern democracy which, for the first time, authorised itself to invent and not only to interpret (religion or customs).

Modernity and democracy initiate the liberation of the individual and beyond, potentially, of society. But they only initiate it, because they remain fettered by the requirements of capitalist reproduction. However, this beginning is not without importance, far from it. Democracy enables social struggles (class struggles) to make themselves felt, to flourish and perhaps to make possible a decisive transformation, the concept of socialism – beyond capitalism – and the freedom to struggle with this perspective.

At the same time, modernity and democracy transform the state and politics, where the conflicts take place both around power and around the linking of its exercise to social interests, which are themselves in conflict on their own grounds. The complexity of political struggle thus becomes a major reality. It produces a differentiation and a multiplication of representations of reality and issues by the actors, who are themselves subject to permanent differentiation and multiplication of representations.

Marx, as Garo has powerfully demonstrated, was very careful about the complex interferences of perceptions, of systems of

7 BEING MARXIST, BEING COMMUNIST, BEING INTERNATIONALIST

general or particular ideas (ideologies) in a specific field of social and/or political struggle (or both at the same time).

When treating this subject he used a vocabulary which has a broad range of terms. Garo cites 16 of them: appearance, representation, presentation, abstraction, expression, signification, ideology, fiction, reflection, analogy, vision, fetishism, illusion, method, intellectual production, imagination (Garo 2000, p. 268).

Marx, critic of social thought, and the centrality of 'representation'

Marx was not a philosopher, an economist, a sociologist, a historian. He was not even a scholar who possessed all these fields of knowledge. He was more than that: the critic of philosophy, of political economy, of sociology, of representations of history. He was the critic of social thought that based its formulations on the different segments of knowledge brought together from these fields.

All these specialised fields of knowledge (economics, social history, political history) or generalised fields (philosophy) share in common representations of reality or what they claim it to be. Thus they are intellectual productions.

Philosophy itself, and all the philosophies, are representations. Whether it is Greek philosophy or that of the Enlightenment and of classical Europe, or of modern philosophers (after Marx), they are all intellectual productions and therefore cannot be understood outside the social reality (the historical economic and social formation, to which I shall return later) within which they were formulated.

It is the same for the religions that have taken the place of philosophy (and still do). They are representations that have found their place as representations of the universe, of society and of the human being in the social formations in which they were constituted. They have even been, I believe, *the* major and fundamental representations that conform to the needs of the reproduction of social formations that I have described as 'tributary', preceding capitalist modernity. But they have also proved their flexibility, that is their capacity to reinterpret themselves to survive the transformations of social formations. In that respect they share with many representations (if not all of them) the capacity to evolve by themselves. These evolutions are ordered both by their own internal logic and by that governing the social formation as a whole. This coming together is fruitful, or not, possible or not, advantageous and positive or negative, depending on the case (I shall return to this question later, which I have described as 'under-determination').

The same applies to philosophies or systems of thought in other, non-European societies. Confucianism is a representation. It has even been a powerful and flexible representation – powerful because flexible. After its first, original formulation it was reconciled with Buddhism, under the Tangs, especially, then it was reformulated, during the Song and Ming dynasties, before the western intrusion into China's history, in a spirit that was firmly initiating modernity, with the abolition of the (Buddhist) state religion and the invention of the first secularism.

At this time, Chinese philosophy developed before the Enlightenment (which, in fact, it inspired much more than is generally believed). Confucianism even found a new role in the effort of modern nationalist China to reconcile it with capitalism – unfortunate, in my opinion – the failure of which opened up the way to the penetration of Marxism/Maoism and communism into Chinese thinking and action. Reconciliation, with a view to its restoration in our post-Maoist epoch? It is a serious and important question. This Confucianism (or pseudo-Confucianism, whatever it is) is still the dominant ideology in Taiwan and partially in Japan (in a version deformed by being grafted onto Shintoism) and in Korea.

What I have said here about philosophy as (general) representation is also valid for the segmented representations, particularly political economy and political ideologies (liberalism and others).

Marx wanted not only to criticise representations. He also wanted to criticise first, reality, then its representation and finally its practices, starting with the choices of action that the actors of history made based on their representations. These three dimensions of the critique are inseparable for Marx.

The aim of the criticism of reality is primordial. By that Marx meant that a correct representation of reality is possible. The discovery – gradual – of the reality of what societies have really

7 BEING MARXIST, BEING COMMUNIST, BEING INTERNATIONALIST

been and are, yesterday and today, constitutes his first permanent concern. In other words, Marx thought that representation could become scientific, that is, making it possible to discover the actual reality. He proposed a formulation (his own 'intellectual production'), based on the abstract concept of historical social formation. This formulation is, in my humble opinion, greatly superior – whatever its limitations – to all the other 'theories' of society and history that have been proposed up until now.

To achieve it, Marx made two choices. One was for materialism: that is, the existence of a reality outside (and before) its representation, which may be correct (perhaps partially) or not at all (illusionary).

The other was for dialectics: the reality itself is inseparable from its movement, ordered by the contradiction – A and B in conflict – and its resolution by the invention of C, which is neither the triumph of A over B or vice versa, nor a new mixture of the two. This materialist dialectic (a term I prefer to 'dialectic materialism') qualitatively goes beyond formal logic. I refer here to what I have written on the subject in *From Capitalism to Civilization* (2010).

The result of Marx implementing this method (the work of Marx) should be given the serious consideration it merits. In historical Marxism it is all too often considered as the final result: there was nothing to be added, nothing to be corrected. I disagree: my point of view is that to be Marxist is to start from Marx, not stop with him.

Marx was not content just with criticising reality and its representations. He observed that human beings, individually and collectively, were permanently engaged in acting, transforming and wanting to transform reality. They did so on the basis and by means of the representations that they had of this reality. Even the 'conservatives', who claimed not to want change, acted, even if only to try to hinder the change. Marx saw this as a permanent task and chose his camp, not only, for completely respectable moral and human reasons, that of the oppressed and exploited (who would dare to say that they do not exist!); also he chose the camp of those who aim to change the world by helping them to deliver what his movement ambitiously aimed at: the abolition of oppression and exploitation, as well as of classes, and the replacement of capitalism by communism, which was necessary (in the sense that the movement went in that direction) and therefore possible.

This choice, which I wholeheartedly agree with, does, however, pose three series of questions that have to be faced.

First: emancipation, envisaged as the communist future, defines itself as the freedom from alienation, which is at the origin of the distance separating representations of the world from its reality. For my part, I have proposed a classification listing these alienations in distinct, superimposed categories and I opted for a modest solution: communism allows a society to get rid of the economist/market alienation, which is itself the condition that enables the reproduction of the capitalist system, but perhaps not also the alienations that I have described as anthropological. I refer the reader to these developments which I proposed in *Unequal Development* (1976).

Second: as capitalism develops it produces its 'gravedigger' (the proletariat) and the time becomes ripe for the possibility of it being overtaken by communism. But is this inescapable? I would be careful in drawing this conclusion, since in fact Marx does not do so. The collapse, or even self-destruction, of a society is also considered possible. In order to understand and thus define the necessary hypotheses for either the success or the failure of the transformation on the spectrum of the possible/necessary, I suggest the concept of under-determination. In transition periods like ours, there is a host of multiple determinations impacting on the system, pushing it in a direction that can be revolutionary or chaotic (revolution or decadence, as I have put it).

Third: what should be made of the representation of society that Marx's own construction has produced (an intellectual production like the others, that he himself criticised)? Should not Marxism be subjected to critical Marxism? Marx never avoided this question. The representation that he proposed is not a closed and definitive theory (Marxism) but an ensemble of open questions, with no closure being possible. I do not believe that the attempt made by Karl Mannheim (1952) in *Ideology and Utopia* helps us to progress on this question because he is making a – remarkable – criticism of historical Marxism, not of Marx.

7 BEING MARXIST, BEING COMMUNIST, BEING INTERNATIONALIST

Marx: critic of capitalist reality and its bourgeois representation

Marx never separated his tireless research into the actual reality of capitalism – both its basis in the capitalist economy as well as the way in which it functioned politically, in which were entangled class struggles (in the plural as they were not limited to the central bourgeoisie/proletariat struggle) – and political conflicts. Marx gradually discovered this reality, that of the historical social formation of capitalism, through dissecting the representations that it gave itself.

I would add that the reality that Marx wanted to understand (to make the struggle more effective for the positive overthrow of capitalism) is both the economic laws that generate its reproduction (I would prefer to say requirements rather than laws, which imply a determinism that is foreign to Marx's thinking) and the way in which its political form is deployed. These two faces of reality are inseparable.

I also share the viewpoint of Garo, who saw no contradiction between the concrete historical analyses of French politics between 1848 and 1871, and the theses of *Capital*, as has been wrongly suggested by Raymond Aron, who is not well equipped to understand the spirit of Marx's research in the way he artificially divides Marx into 'economist', 'sociologist' and 'political actor'.

Marx thus produced a critique of political economy, the essential subtitle of *Capital*, which was a critique of the economic discourse of capitalism. And it is in this sense that *Capital* should be read, not as good economic science, as opposed to bad (or imperfect) economic science of others (classical or popular). Rather *Capital* was the discovery of the existence of this representation used by the bourgeois political economy, in its origins and in its (active) functions in reproducing its system.

But it was also a study of capitalism's limits, its internal contradictions that it cannot overcome, and of its character that is, finally, not scientific but ideological. The term 'ideology' should be understood here in one of the senses that Marx gave it: not simply as a system of ideas, a vision, a 'Weltanschauung' (construction of the world), but in its pejorative sense of false consciousness, illusion, a masking of the alienations that condition the formulations.

The to-ing and fro-ing from the concrete to the abstract, from apparent phenomena to the hidden essence, constitute the living body of materialist dialectics in operation. Work, value, goods thus become forms of discovered abstraction which makes it possible to define capital as the social relationship, the surplus labour and the exploitation that originate in the mode of production (and not in the circulation and distribution of income). The shift from the abstract (the capitalist mode of production) to the concrete (social formation) thus integrates the forms produced by the genesis of historical capitalism (ownership of land, rent), those forms produced by the requirements of its political management (the state, political economies, the management of credit and currency) and those produced by the enrolment of each of these social formations of historical capitalism into the globalised capitalist system (foreign trade).

The result of this effort is remarkable but also unequalled. All the bourgeois economic science subsequent to Marx, even the most sophisticated of modern times, even the most critical (like that of Keynes) make, in my humble opinion, a poor showing compared with the monumental *Capital*.

That does not mean that the result is final – it cannot be. This is not only because Marx did not have the time to complete it, but because the very idea of its completion was alien to Marx's mind and method.

Marx was, after all, somewhat limited by his times. He did not take a miraculous medicine that vaccinated him against the errors and especially all the illusions and visions of his times. He did not claim to be infallible, even if his interpretation by historical Marxism sometimes implies it.

I myself have dared to propose continuing this critique of the political economy by restoring the whole extent of the challenge constituted by the world capitalist system. Thus I propose extending the theory of value at the most abstract level of its formulation (in the mode of capitalist production, itself an abstraction) towards formulating the 'law of globalised value'. This has been the central object of my research for half a century. I now realise, with the advantage of hindsight, that in order to do it I

7 BEING MARXIST, BEING COMMUNIST, BEING INTERNATIONALIST

benefited from being outside the centre (developed capitalism) in the peripheries (the very result of globalised capitalism), with a viewpoint that I thus hope was free from Eurocentrism. I also could not do it other than nowadays, after Marx, in our epoch of the capitalism of the oligopolies. And in doing it I benefited from the lead of Lenin in this field.

The conclusion that Marx came to, and to which I subscribe, is that the bourgeois political economy, which had become vulgar (see Translator's note) by necessity (as it continues to be), is an ideology in the strictest sense of the word: a functional representation, as Garo says, that is directly of use to 'ownership', by legitimising its claimed necessity. This implies, right from the beginning, that bourgeois political economy analyses only the immediate realities through which economic life expresses itself. The capitalist takes profits in proportion to the capital that he puts to work, therefore the capital is productive. When I recalled, in my book *From Capitalism to Civilization* (2010), the productivity of social labour, erased by today's left-wing economists (even those who claim to be Marxists!), I was just pointing out that the representation of the economy that they propose remains a vulgar representation.

It is not surprising that a – positivist – Marxian political economy has replaced Marx's critique of the political economy. That this trend has mainly been produced by Anglo-American academics, before being adopted by others, is understandable given the attachment to empiricism that characterises their culture. The false question of the transformation of value into price is an example.

The transformation implies a rate of profit expressed in the system of production prices that is different from the rate of profit expressed in the system of values. Marxians see an 'error' here that abolishes the validity of the law of value. However, according to Marx's thinking, there is no contradiction and still less an error: the rate of apparent profit (expressed in the pricing system) must be different from its real rate, itself directly associated to the rate of surplus value that measures the exploitation of work. Science always involves going beyond appearances, as Marx said many times. For our economists, who are bogged down in empiricism, knowledge is reduced to what is immediately apparent. I insist on this point, which is never understood by our Marxians who have, alas, established a school of thought on the European continent.

I have also proposed reading the Marx of historical Marxism of the 20th century (the Marxism of Soviet planning) and the Keynes of the social democracy of the welfare state as two representations (both of them deformed) of reality: that of the Soviet society and that of the post-war western societies. And however much Keynes was an authentic genius, his economics remains commonplace. Of course it was of a banality that was different from that of the liberals. But his concept of a preference for liquidity and the marginal efficiency of capital stems directly from his reading of the appearances by which the reproduction of capital manifests itself.

The sophistication of modern economics, originating from North American universities, does not succeed in hiding the banality of the method that reveals the fundamental empiricism on which it is based. It is a method that proposes to collect together the 'facts' (that is, the facts as they are presented in the immediate picture), then search the correlations among them to establish the 'laws'.

The way this vulgar economics functions is, to me, blindingly obvious to the point of being able to compare this function to the discourses of the sorcerers of ancient times (pure economics or the witchcraft of the contemporary world). Listening to the speeches made at Davos in 2009, with the economists practising all kinds of contortions as they talked about the crisis being 'unexpected', 'unexplained', 'inexplicable', I felt vindicated in my views.

The representation of the economic discourse (from the political economy in the times of Marx to the pure economics of our days) is certainly an active discourse that shapes the reproduction of the system. It is not a useless bit of décor. Not only do business leaders believe in its scientific reality, but general opinion believes it just as much. Both expect governments to be inspired by the 'scientific' knowledge that this representation produces for finding the solution to the problems – these days, the financial crisis, unemployment and so on.

Economic policy thus constitutes the active result of this representation. I am not saying that this economic policy is necessarily and always ineffective. The knowledge on which it is based can, to a certain degree, be reliable. Proof is given from time to time

7 BEING MARXIST, BEING COMMUNIST, BEING INTERNATIONALIST

by the effectiveness of this or that economic policy. But I would put a damper on this reputation for efficacy. The New Deal, for example, only attenuated the extent of the crisis; it was the Second World War that ended it. It is now known that Hitler's economic policy, which was so praised, was not really effective. One could multiply the examples. Capitalism remains, in fact, a system that is not properly controlled by those who are its active agents (the businessmen) nor by those who, in politics, try to impose some order on it.

Marx also made a critique of politics, of the state and democracy, of political conflicts and of class struggle. His objective was not to write an academic manual of political science, like the well-known philosopher Raymond Aron. He developed a method for the critique of politics which was the same as for his critique of capitalism.

Just as he had chosen England (the beacon country for the development of the capitalist economy in his time) to make a critique of political economy, he selected France for his critique of politics. For it was France that had invented the state and the modern politics of capitalism. The English revolution of 1640, then the far from glorious revolution of 1688 and the non-revolution called the American War of Independence, were certainly innovatory, but they went only half way. It was the French Revolution that invented modern politics and, with it, the modern state. It was a great revolution and a genuine one, because it envisaged the long-term objective needs of its times, as later the Russian and Chinese revolutions were to do. The drama of the great revolutions explains also their later retreats and the untiring pursuit of political conflicts entangled with the class conflicts that constitute modern politics.

The particular attention that Marx gave to France was thus deliberate. It was on the basis of his reading of the political conflicts and social struggles in France that Marx was able to make his critique of the state and of politics and discover (or approach, to be modest, as Marx was) the reality of the state and modern politics. The subjects chosen by Marx, the revolution of 1848, the Eighteenth Brumaire of Louis Napoleon (his *coup d'état* of 1851), the Paris Commune were not selected by chance, as Raymond Aron would have it. They are no less fundamental than *Capital* in understanding both the reality of the capitalist social formation in its integrality (that is, as an economic, political, and social entity) and the nature of the representations that the actors in history made of them.

Marx therefore set to disentangling the muddle of the discourses (representations) of the actors in this historical period and in the class struggles. He forgot none of these representations and gave them their full force in explaining the choices of action and the results that were produced. He gave their rightful place to the heirs of Jacobinism and 'the Mountain', to the *Blanquistes*, to the heralds of the business bourgeoisie (Guizot and others), to the political adventurers (Louis Napoleon Bonaparte), to the spokesmen of the workers who were organising, to the peasantry who were apparently silent, and even to insignificant personalities (such as Lamartine). Later, with the creation of the International Working Men's Association, then the Paris Commune, 'the ascent to attack the sky', he crossed swords with the anarcho-communist representations of Bakunin, the hesitant ideas of Proudhon, the state theories of Lassale, the narrow-mindedness of English trade unionism.

The theory of the state outlined by Marx and Engels and later by Lenin, and those of democracy and modern politics, are the result of this critique. Or, more exactly, Marx, Engels and Lenin set down the bases of this theory which, like that of capital, cannot be completed, either theoretically or in practice. For these analyses must always be up for question, rethought and reformulated. And the state and politics pursue their evolution and change with the permanent transformation of the capitalist reality.

The contrast between this analysis of the new reality made by Marx and the prodigious analysis made by Machiavelli of the ancient political reality should impress the attentive reader. Machiavelli speaks about the reality of another time, another kind of power.

The critique of politics and of the state proposed by Marx is both fundamental for the whole history of capitalism, including its latest developments, and limited by its period. This critique should have been pursued, as Lenin did, but he only started it. This has not been the case for historical Marxism which became bogged down, repeating what Marx had said in his time.

I tried to continue this critique in *The Liberal Virus* (2004).

7 BEING MARXIST, BEING COMMUNIST, BEING INTERNATIONALIST

The Liberal Virus

What I tried to do in my recent work with this title (it had an important subtitle: *Permanent War and the Americanization of the World*) was to update the dominant discourse (the representation) of our globalised neoliberalism, which is now in open crisis.

The critique of this discourse is based on a representation (mine) of the reality of capitalism today. It continues to be capitalism and therefore the essence of what Marx said about it remains perfectly valid: work and exploitation, commercial alienation and expansion, the fetishism of money, false representations of the (alienated) individual and of competition, the state at the service of capital, the alienated representations of political actors (illusions of democracy), the entanglement of social struggles and political conflicts. I do not hesitate however in 'completing' these representations and their critique as Marx proposed them for his time, stressing what is new in contemporary capitalism.

The Liberal Virus therefore combines two discourses, two representations: that of the new pure economics (the modern form of vulgar economics) and that of the model American democracy. These are two discourses that are very useful in serving, and giving the appearance of legitimacy to, the domination of the oligopolies in the centres that have become the collective imperialism of the Triad (United States, Europe, Japan) and at world level (through the militarisation of globalisation and the 'compradorisation' of the governing classes of the peripheries). These discourses are less scientific than ever, purely ideological, but nevertheless active. They are the expression of the decline of bourgeois thought, the end of the Enlightenment.

The liberal virus expresses itself through the separation of the management of the economy and the political management of society; the reduction of economic rationality to the myth of generalised markets that tend to produce a general equilibrium (even optimal because they respond to the preferences of individuals); the dissociation of political management, reduced to electoral representative and multiparty democracy, from questions of social progress; the limitation of human rights which cannot cross the limits of the supreme value of private property; the description of globalisation as positively global.

These ideas are developed further in *The Liberal Virus*. I shall just emphasise that liberal philosophy evades the essence of historical capitalism in general, and of the actually existing (see Translator's note) capitalism of today, in particular.

Capitalism has become a capitalism of oligopolies that dominate the whole productive and financial system. The dominant class at the world level, which corresponds to this concentration of capital (unprecedented compared with previous stages of capitalism's history), is composed of a veritable plutocracy which, for this reason, has become the enemy of all humanity. Oligarchy is not restricted to Russia, as we are led to believe. It is no less real in the United States, Europe and Japan.

This system is financialised in the sense that the monetary and financial market (itself globalised) has become the dominant market that, in turn, structures all the other markets that govern labour, access to natural resources and production outlets.

The liberal discourse thus makes it impossible to understand why the present crisis began with the collapse of the monetary and financial market, the Achilles heel of the system. It was perfectly predictable (but not by the conventional economists) because it is a systemic crisis of ageing capitalism which is obsolete and senile. In addition, this discourse eliminates the centre–periphery contradiction, which is inherent in the (imperialist) polarising expansion of globalised historical capitalism. These days this erasure is particularly the expression of the new monopolies based on the domination of the centres (control of technology, access to natural resources, global financialisation, communications and information, weapons of mass destruction), which now substitute for the ancient privilege of the exclusive industrialisation of the centres.

The centre–periphery conflict is exacerbated by the new conditions created by natural resources becoming relatively rare, which gives the conflict over their control at world level a decisive dimension in the geopolitics/geostrategics of the centres.

The liberal virus comes from a political culture of consensus, which is based on eliminating the reality of social classes and nations, proclaiming the individual as the subject of history.

7 BEING MARXIST, BEING COMMUNIST, BEING INTERNATIONALIST

In my books *Obsolescent Capitalism* (2003) and *Spectres of Capitalism* (1998), I emphasised the transformations in the economic dimensions of modern capitalism. In *The Liberal Virus*, I stressed the political dimensions. But the two critiques cannot be separated. In other words, the capitalism of the oligopolies, the deepening globalisation, financialisation, the crisis of the model of economic management (collapse of the financial markets, the ongoing depression), the systemic crisis (of energy, of food/agriculture, climate change, destruction of the peasantry, the growing scarcity of natural resources), the decline in the credibility of democracy, the rise in nostalgic illusions, the illusions of the individual (the king that he is not), the 'single party of the oligopolies', the collective imperialism of the Triad, the relative and absolute pauperisation at the world level, the militarisation of globalisation, the race to control the natural resources of the planet, apartheid at the world level: all these together constitute the portrait of reality that the economist/liberal representation leaves out of its considerations. The other discourses, the representations that the movements in struggle have of reality, are on the whole fragmented – that is, they generally concern only one of the dimensions of the total reality, whose elements are spelt out above.

The Americanisation of this renewed functional representation must be emphasised. The contrast I wanted to make between the European political culture(s) and that of the United States is, in my humble opinion, essential for understanding the fatal dangers that the Americanisation of Europe entails. It closes the door on a gradual transformation along the road to socialism and opens the way to a continually growing chaos which could become even worse, leading to the self-destruction of civilisation.

The debate on democracy in America is certainly not new. I have taken a position against the reactionary comments of de Tocqueville and the spinelessness of Raymond Aron, both of them technologists, for whom the industrial society replaces the capitalist society. I even expressed an opinion which is not that of Marx, who admired the North American capitalism 'free of feudal vestiges'. My thesis is that the more capitalism is pure, the stronger the correlation will be between the needs for the reproduction of the power of capital (today that of the oligopolies) and the expressions of the political representation that suits it. Consensus closes the door to a socialist consciousness.

Europe – starting with France – thus invented one modern political (and state) form, while the United States has quite another.

The great revolutions carried out in the name of socialism, those of Russia and China, included in their programme the invention of a new state and a new politics, that of the transition to socialism. They were well on the way after their victories but later got stuck, even retreating. The first effort to construct a politics for the future has thus aborted. The task of achieving it therefore remains ahead of us.

The other dimension of the functioning of the state and the policies of capitalism is that which I have described as the 'awakening of the South' (the title of the book *L'Éveil du Sud* I produced on the subject in 2008). A result of the victories of national liberation in Asia and Africa after the Second World War and of the Bandung era, it brought about the modernisation of the new state (or the renewal of the old, premodern, pre-colonial state) and a flourishing political life that had been unknown in those societies, and which was obviously associated with the development programmes initiated to leave behind the night of domination by the old, colonial and semi-colonial imperialism. I have tried here, inspired largely by lessons drawn from my readings of Marx, of historical Marxists and others, to disentangle the new muddle of the social struggles, the power conflicts and their ideological representations.

What is new here about the state, politics and democracy as regards the first advances of Marx in these fields? There are the old and the permanent elements that are particular to capitalism, but there are also new ones.

The state remains a class state: in the final analysis it is always the servant of property, of capital. Bourgeois democracy reinforces this character, defined as it is by its representative form whether parliamentary (in the European tradition which is in the process of being eroded) or presidential (the clever invention of the Founding Fathers, aware of its power to destroy the potential danger of democracy). Universal suffrage, which came late and upon which Marx based some hope, did not threaten the power of

7 BEING MARXIST, BEING COMMUNIST, BEING INTERNATIONALIST

capital (as I observed in my 2001 article 'Marx et la démocratie'), as it was associated with the emergence of social imperialism, to which I shall return.

Neither did multipartyism, which also developed later, largely in response to the formation of workers' parties, seriously challenge the power of capital. Nor did the recognition of many and expanded rights, even including some social rights, but all of them forbidden from crossing the red line of the right to property. These democratic advances were not made from a perspective of the transition to socialism but, on the contrary, reinforced bourgeois democracy in what was most essential, its association with the power of the bourgeoisie. Nevertheless they shaped a political life that saw the multiplication of conflicts over the exercise of power. These conflicts have always been dispersed and fragmented, producing and mobilising endless discourses (of representation), which are themselves fragmented. The entanglement of these conflicts with class struggles in this way weakened the revolutionary potential of the latter and blocked the way to a socialist transition.

Today, with the strengthening of the power of the oligopolies in the economic field, the state is more than ever the state of the capital of these oligopolies. One must not therefore be surprised at the way it is managing political democracy towards less democracy and more consensus, as in the United States.

Nevertheless this state of capital can also be a social state. The social-democratic historical compromise of capital and labour during the post–Second World War period is an excellent example. But, as I observed above, this compromise, which was imposed by the defeat of fascism and the legitimacy gained from this by the working-class parties, was possible only thanks to imperialist rent.

There is something new in the peripheries of the system because here the functional state for dominant imperialist capital is the comprador state. There is no shortage of models from previous epochs: the Ottoman sultan, the Egyptian khedive, the shah of Iran, the emperor of China, the *latifundista* states of Latin America. This kind of state has its local social base in the classes that benefit from imperialist expansion: old feudalists converted into agrarian semi-capitalism and the intermediary bourgeoisie (the compradores in the strict sense of the term). These models can hardly accommodate bourgeois democracy. New forms of the comprador state have been invented in more recent times in independent Africa (described as neocolonial) and they too are incapable of respecting the minimal requirements of bourgeois democracy.

For those very reasons, the comprador state has never been able to acquire the stability of the states of capital in the imperialist centres. It has been completely overturned by revolutions under the banner of socialism and Marxism (that became Marxism-Leninism) in Russia, China, Vietnam and Cuba. Or it has been seriously transformed, in various degrees, by nationalist, popular (see Translator's note) blocs for national liberation.

In the periphery the entanglement of conflicts around power and class struggles has been no less complex than in the contemporary centres. The subordination of radical class struggles to other objectives, said or claimed to be derived from the needs of development, is also visible. But this entanglement takes on a different form from that of the centres. For here, the conflicts to acquire power – to make it possible to gain access to the ownership of capital – have had to be presented in other ways. Particular representations have given expression to these conflicts, giving credibility and legitimacy to their discourses. I have tried to disentangle the threads of some of these entanglements for the countries of Asia and Africa during the Bandung era in *L'Éveil du Sud*.

To sum up, what I think is worth remembering from these contributions, which I believe absolutely to be Marxist and not neo-Marxist, is the emphasis on the world dimension of actually existing historical capitalism/imperialism. This dimension may even have been underestimated by Marx himself. In any case it was abolished by the historical Marxism of the Second International and the social-imperialists that built it. It was half reinstated by the Third International, to be sidelined subsequently by the constraints of the need for coexistence advocated by the Soviet Union (not by the imperialist powers). These ideas were taken much further by Maoism.

Historical Marxism (or all these Marxisms, to different degrees) always tends to reduce the world system to a juxtaposition of capitalist formations (or formations on their way to becoming

7 BEING MARXIST, BEING COMMUNIST, BEING INTERNATIONALIST

capitalist), whether or not they were unequally developed and thus eventually overpowered. I have taken a systematic opposition to this viewpoint and sought to understand the world system in a different way, as consisting of centres and peripheries that are inseparable from each other.

In this perspective, the concepts of the globalised law of value and its corollary, the imperialist rent, enrich the decisive and determining advances by Marx. They do not negate them – on the contrary.

This is because what Marx had derived from his construction (capitalist reality) is, at the level of the world system, strikingly confirmed by the facts. The centre–periphery polarisation is simply another way of describing a gigantic pauperisation, relative and absolute, on an even greater scale than Marx had envisaged in his epoch.

The accelerated growth of proletarianisation at one end (in the peripheries), associated with its apparent decrease in the centres (I say apparent because what I call the general proletarianisation takes on other forms) also confirms the views of Marx.

Taking into account the globalisation of capital, as must be done, enriches the range of representations that guide the action of the social forces that are in struggle. These specific discourses are important, and sometimes decisive because the contrast between centres and peripheries entails the involvement of classes and nations (and peoples). In the centres this entanglement is inseparable from the imperialist rent and its effects on the whole society (and not only on the volume of capital's profits). In the peripheries it gives the objective of national independence new scope.

To give the imperialist reality of capitalism all the importance it should have means introducing geopolitical/geostrategic conflicts into the analysis of the requirements of the reproduction of economic and political reality and translating them into active representations, as it also requires dividing capitalist expansion into significant phases.

The geopolitics of capitalism/imperialism in crisis

The main theme that I have put forward on this subject is that imperialism, which was once referred to in the plural, has now become the collective imperialism of the Triad. This qualitative transformation corresponds exactly to the degree of capital concentration mentioned earlier.

Nevertheless, its political management remains mostly national (even within the European Union, and all the more so in the Triad countries as a whole), hence there is a possible contradiction between the economic management of the globalised, financialised system by collective imperialism and its political management by the states of the Triad.

However, I stress that it was possible to reconcile globalised economic management and national political management during the whole period of neoliberal ascent (1980–2008). This reconciliation reduced the extent of possible intra-Atlantic conflicts between Europe and the United States and intra-European conflicts within the European Union. Beyond this, it attenuated the North–South conflicts in that the emerging countries of the South aligned themselves with the requirements of globalisation and even, by accelerating their growth, obtained some short-term profits from it, while other countries of the South were forced to submit passively to these requirements.

This page of history has now been turned with the onset of the globalisation crisis, starting with its financial crisis.

New questions thus arise: will the development of the crisis lead to a weakening of Atlanticism, to its revision, or to its breakup? Or, perhaps, to its reinforcement? The European Union and, within it, the euro zone: are they destined to explode? to stagnate? or to be strengthened? Is the conflict between imperialism and the main emerging countries – in particular China, but also Russia, and perhaps others – likely to become more acute? Or will everyone accommodate themselves to viable compromises in the crisis? Will the other countries of the Third World escape their lethargy, or sink deeper into it?

The replies to these questions, which are necessarily diverse, will depend both on ongoing struggles and those to come: social struggles (local dominated classes against dominating classes) in all their political dimensions, international conflicts between the leading blocs in command positions of the states and nations. There are no evident prognoses and different ones are possible. This does not exclude but indeed requires the concrete analysis of all these contradictions and the conflicts that they create.

The division of capitalist expansion into significant phases

There are different ways of making this division, depending on the main criteria that need to be stressed.

The 'economicist' tradition is technologist in the sense that it identifies the divisions in terms of the main technological revolutions of modern history. This has some validity. But it is necessary to put this approach into perspective and above all not to take a technological stance: that technology decides everything (that it will be, at last resort, the motor of history) and that the rest will adjust to its requirements. Kondratieff cycles can be reconciled to a technological and economicist interpretation (successive phases of expansion and stagnation, inflationary and deflationary phases, etc). I will not repeat the criticisms I have made of such interpretations. The cycles of hegemonies (the United Provinces, Great Britain, United States) are dear to Wallerstein, to Arrighi and, to some extent, to Gunder Frank. I refer here to my criticisms of this succession of stages, which seem to me to be forced.

Gramsci proposed long political cycles, defined by the composition of the hegemonic alliances that shaped the economic and social conditions of capitalist reproduction. As an example he put forward, as far as France was concerned, the two phases 1789–1870 then 1870–1930, which he saw as successive phases of the stabilisation of bourgeois hegemony, in conflict with the still strong vestiges of the hegemonies of the Ancien Régime. The first phase was a competitive capitalism; the second, that of the monopolies (here Gramsci takes up the writings of Lenin). The hegemonic alliances that characterise each of these phases are specific: during the first the bourgeoisie made concessions to the forces of the Ancien Régime (the aristocracy, the church) and kept down the peasantry who came out of the revolution, in order to isolate the new working class; in the second, it made historical compromises with the waged classes.

I don't hide my conviction that the method that Gramsci proposes is sounder than the others, in the sense that he stressed the essential forces that shape the transformation: the class struggle.

I have tried to use this method to characterise the specific political cultures of the main imperialist nations, emphasising the original compromise, sometimes a serious one, between the bourgeoisie and the political forces of the *anciens régimes*. I have also tried to implement this method in my analyses concerning the centre–periphery conflict, characterising the centres by their capacity to implement the capital/labour historical compromise in late mature capitalism (the welfare state) and hence 'social imperialism'. And I have shown the incapacity of the bourgeoisie in the peripheries, because of their compradorisation, to construct a stable capitalism.

As we know, Lenin believed that there had been a rupture (at the end of the 19th century) between rising, competitive capitalism and the capitalism/imperialism of the monopolies, which had entered into the age of its destructive senility, thus putting the socialist revolution on the agenda. I subscribe to this thesis but would put it into perspective.

The division I would make in the modern period of capitalism is based on the idea that the 20th century saw the first great phase (I call it 'wave') of the progress of struggles by the workers and peoples.

The century, in turn, divides into successive moments.

From 1890 to 1914 there was a first belle époque (liberal financialised globalisation based on the several imperialisms) which led to the inter-imperialist war and the Russian Revolution. This belle époque was itself the response to the great systemic crisis which had preceded it, from 1873 to the end of the century.

To leave behind this first failure of generalised liberalism, the dominant powers from 1920 set to restoring the belle époque, which led to the great crisis and the Second World War. The period is also that of the 30 Years War between the United States and Germany for succession to the hegemony of Great Britain.

The war ended in victory for democracy over fascism, victory of the Red Army, of the worker parties and of the anti-colonial movements. There were new conditions, with the working classes

7 BEING MARXIST, BEING COMMUNIST, BEING INTERNATIONALIST

and the colonial peoples having gained a respectability that they had never had before. This made possible, between 1945 and 1980, the establishment of the welfare state in the countries of the imperialist Triad (social imperialism), the second great revolution (in China) and the victory of the national liberation struggles in Africa and Asia (the Bandung era).

These post-war models were worn out by 1980, after the new systemic crisis which began as of 1968–1971, and this made it possible to dream of a return to generalised liberalism (associated this time with the collective imperialism of the Triad). So then we entered into a second belle époque, introducing a possible and desirable second wave of struggles for the emancipation of humanity.

Thus it is that history repeats itself, quite obviously to me, and I have analysed it in these terms from the end of the 1980s.

The page is now turned of this second belle époque (1980–2008), which was based on the collective imperialism of the Triad, the erosion then collapse of the Soviet Union, the passage to post-Maoism in China, the collapse of the national popular models of Bandung and the social-liberal drift (see Translator's note) of social democracy. This does not mean that the oligarchies are not trying to restore it.

The liberal ideologues saw financialised globalisation as the 'end of history'. Personally I thought from the beginning that it was unstable and unviable, as I said earlier. The event surprised the liberals, but not myself and some others – very few, alas, at that time.

The development of struggles from 1995 onwards shows the social and political dimension of this instability: the financial collapse of October 2008 and its incapacity to overcome the internal contradictions of its mode of economic management. I shall come back to the importance that should be given to these two modes of system collapse, that is, through internal contradictions or through the victorious struggles of the victims (see the conclusion to *Class and Nation* 1980). From 2008 we have been confronted with questions about the future that can be resolved only by the development and radicalisation of the current struggles.

The social struggles and political conflicts of today

Today, just as in the past, the struggles to transform society and political conflict are most certainly not unconnected. All social demands, however modest, become the object of political conflict and none of them can continue indefinitely without having a social impact.

Nevertheless, it is useful to distinguish between these two aspects of reality, even if they are two sides of the same coin. We could start with the diversity of aspirations that motivate mobilisations and social struggles and perhaps divide these aspirations into five groups: for political democracy and respect for individual rights and freedom; for social justice; for respect for diverse groups and communities; for better ecological management; for obtaining a better position in the world system.

Clearly the protagonists of movements that stand for these aspirations are rarely the same. For example, the concern that one's country should obtain a higher position in the world hierarchy, defined in terms of wealth, power and autonomy of action, is primarily a concern of the governing classes, of those in power, rather than of the people as a whole even though it would have their backing. The aspiration for respect – in the fullest meaning of the word, that is for really equal treatment – can mobilise women round their position as women, or a cultural, linguistic or religious group that is discriminated against. These movements can be trans-class.

On the other hand, the aspiration for more social justice, defined variously, depending on the different movements – for greater material well-being, for legislation that is more appropriate and efficacious, or for a system of social relations and production that is radically different – all these almost necessarily involve the class struggle. It can be the demand of the peasantry or of one of its sectors for an agrarian reform, a redistribution of property, a legislation that favours, for example, tenants or better prices. It can be for union rights, employment legislation, or even the need for state politics that makes its intervention on behalf of workers more effective – to the point of nationalisation, co-management and worker management. But it can also be the

7 BEING MARXIST, BEING COMMUNIST, BEING INTERNATIONALIST

demands of professional or entrepreneurial groups claiming a reduction in taxes. It can be demands concerning the people as a whole, like the movements in favour of the right to education, health or lodging and, *mutatis mutandis*, to appropriate environmental management. The democratic aspiration can be limited and precise, particularly when it is inspiring a movement fighting against a non-democratic power. But it can also be inclusive and thus seen as the lever that makes it possible to bring together all the social demands and claims.

A chart of the actual distribution of these movements would certainly show how tremendously unequal they are on the ground. But the chart would, as we know, be perpetually changing because where there is a problem there is almost always a potential movement to find a solution to it.

One needs to be really naive and extraordinarily optimistic to think that these forces acting in very different fields could give the necessary coherence to a movement that would help societies move towards greater justice and democracy. Chaos is part of nature, just as order is. It would require the same naivety to neglect the reactions of the existing powers towards these movements. The geography of the distribution of these powers and the strategies they develop to meet the challenges that face them, at both the local and the international levels, follow different forms of logic from those on which these aspirations are based.

That is to say that there is a possibility of deviations among social movements, of their being instrumentalised and manipulated. These are also realities that could lead them into powerlessness, or to subscribe to a perspective other than their own.

It would perhaps be useful, in the jungle of struggles and conflicts that make those in power oppose the social movements, or that make the powers oppose each other or even make the social movements themselves oppose each other, to create an inventory of the major issues dominating the contemporary scene.

There is no doubt that priority should be given to a careful analysis of the strategies of the oligarchy in the countries of the Triad, the economic interests at stake and the geopolitics and geostrategy of states that are systematically on the defensive. But an inventory should also be made of the strategies of the dominated powers in the existing world system, both in the countries of the former socialist East and those of the South. One could then draw up a chart of the conflicts where the powers oppose each other. These strategies of the dominated powers are used to destroy certain movements or to subordinate them to objectives that are not their own.

One of the most effective ways of doing this is to promote, support and encourage movements other than those listed above and to push them into directions that are convenient for the powers in conflict. Ethnicity and communitarianism on a national or religious basis, among others, are highly appropriate for this purpose because their demands (shallow as they are) take the place of democratic and social aspirations – to the benefit of local powers and/or dominant powers at the world level. Pretences about being 'left wing' are also useful for this purpose.

To work out all these complex issues it is necessary to understand the challenge that contemporary imperialism poses. On that basis, we might hope to take the debate further as well as to conceptualise the requirements of an effective and consistent alternative.

The language of the discourses

To make a critique of the various representations, it is necessary to understand the vocabulary, that used by Marx as well as that used by the liberals.

We know the current terms used in the tradition of worker and socialist struggles, associated with different concepts it is true, but often at least inspired by the writings of Marx – on the state, politics, classes and class struggles, social change, reform and revolution, power and ideology.

These terms have disappeared from the language, even that of many of the movements that are involved in struggle. Other terms have taken their place: civil society, governance, social partners, communities, alternation (i.e. a change in government but no change in policy), consensus, poverty. These substitutions are not innocuous. They entail adhering to the fundamental requirements of capitalist reproduction.

I would therefore propose re-reading Marx and at the same time I refer to my criticism of those who want to replace him.

7 BEING MARXIST, BEING COMMUNIST, BEING INTERNATIONALIST

Proletariat

With Marx the term 'proletarian' has a precise scientific meaning: people who are forced to sell their labour (the only thing they own) to capital. Workers do not use the means of production, which is done by capital, using labour, subordinating and exploiting it.

In this sense the continual expansion of capital is synonymous with that of the process of proletarianisation. The end of the proletariat, that is, the end of labour subordinated to capital, is just nonsense.

Nevertheless, proletarianisation has never been uniform, always multiform at all stages in the capitalist expansion. The formal submission of artisans in the first period of capitalism (the putting out process), that of modern farmers, those of peasantries in the peripheries of the system, that today of the free workers (who believe themselves free) whose numbers have multiplied because of new forms of capitalist organisation, those of the informal workers: these show the diversity of forms of the general proletarianisation. Moreover this diversity is, at least partially, the result of policies implemented by capital and the state at its service to break the front of labour. These policies also allowed the development of representations specific to each of these situations, thus making it more complex to pass from the consciousness of self to the consciousness for self of the general proletariat. The theory/practice of the struggles (always 'spontaneously' sectoral) – and not that of the theory introduced from outside, or so-called 'creative spontaneity' – is the central plank of the class struggle and of its indispensable politicisation, for its own success, both immediate and more long term.

'Farewell to the proletariat', comes from a simplification by historical Marxism, reducing this class to a fragment. This is the Eurocentric, economicist and worker-idealism (workerist) viewpoint of large-scale industry of the 19th century and then of the Fordist factory of the 20th. This was the objective foundation of the worker-oriented viewpoint, its organisation being facilitated by its concentration in the workplace and, on this basis, of the constitution of worker parties and unions.

The political offensive of capital, which developed in the second belle époque and which still continues, aims at fragmenting the labour front into new and supplementary fronts. The contrast between the conditions of the workers that I have described as 'stabilised' and the conditions of those who are not, which I have highlighted (and I have tried to measure the extent of expansion of this group), is a policy, not the natural and unavoidable consequence of the objective evolution of technologies. This policy is now associated with the financialisation of the system. It objective is to create a creditor front, constituted of pensioners benefiting from privatised pension funds (and thus feeling solidarity with capitalism) and, behind them, the 'stabilised' workers. This front is to oppose that of the 'marginalised' (casual labourers, the unemployed, informal workers and so-called free workers).

All these fragments of the general proletariat constitute what I have described as the 'social basis' (as opposed to the 'electoral basis') of socialism. The convergence of their struggles involves recognising the diversity, not only of their fragmented discourses but also – to a certain extent – their immediate interests. An example of this situation is the conflict between the interests of the urban proletariat (in their capacity as consumers of food products) and the proletarianised peasantry (producers of these products). In constructing convergence this reality cannot be transformed without recognising such diversity. As for the fragmentary discourses, they contribute to the volatility of the electoral bases of the parties and movements that claim to be of the left.

At the global level, as has been said, the proletarianisation under way is synonymous with pauperisation, as Marx understood.

Class and struggle

The diversity of the forms of the general proletarianisation make it necessary to analyse the classes and strategies of the struggles.

Should one then replace the expression 'expansion of the general proletariat' (which I support) with the 'popular classes', as distinct from the 'middle classes'?

Bourgeois social theories, which are always confined within strictly empirical methods, are in favour of this shift. The World Bank knows only the immediate form of the reality – the income pyramid. The classification proposed for the socio-professional categories of the French INSEE (National Institute for Statistics

7 BEING MARXIST, BEING COMMUNIST, BEING INTERNATIONALIST

and Economic Studies) is less rudimentary. It makes it possible to correlate the diversity of representations with that of the electoral options. But it still remains empirical in spirit.

It is not evident that, in the long period of the expansion of historical capitalism, the proportion of the middle classes has constantly increased (the fashionable belief) or decreased (as suggested by a definition of proletarianisation which is not that of Marx). There are several phases of expansion (after the Second World War) and contraction (in moments of great crises, such as ours). But, in all cases, the transformations in the composition of these middle classes have always been subordinated to the transformations in the position of the various components of that class in the production system. To simplify: at one time the small independent producers were, in reality, only apparently independent; now the cadres, mostly salaried, the liberal professions and, here and there, particularly in the peripheries, new small producers, are integrated and subordinated to the process of the reproduction of capital.

The growth of the new middle classes at the centre of the system is associated with imperialist rent. André Gunder Frank and I envisaged, from 1974, the possibility of a new division of labour between the centres and the peripheries. This would be based on the concentration of production at the centre linked to the monopolies through which its domination is expressed at world level (research and technology, armaments, communications, commanding financial systems) and the emigration to the peripheries of the common industrial production, subordinated and dominated through these means. Today this has become reality, confirming our early intuitions. Imperialist rent, appropriated through these monopolies and reinforced by the siphoning off of the natural resources of the planet through their monopoly of access to them, thus transforms the structures of the classes and the representations associated with them.

The structure of the middle classes of the peripheries has also undergone permanent change. But here there are some particularities that are due to the evolution of global capitalism.

The integration of the peasantries of the peripheral regions into the global system has produced a wide variety of transformation, such as the new classes benefiting from imperialist expansion (the *latifundista* of Latin America, Asia and the Arab world, the new 'rich' peasants, the old chieftaincies now converted) as well as the victims (landless peasants and peasants with minuscule plots). New or renewed urbanisation has also seen the emergence of new classes: the compradors profiting from the system, the popular classes that are victims of it, and various middle strata.

Faced by the diversity of situations, amplified by the discourses and representations, is it possible to imagine the emergence of a front of the popular classes (which are the general proletariat with its diverse constituent parts)?

In the centres, one might think that imperialist rent, which aligned social democracy with social imperialism almost from the beginning of the setting up of the modern left, would make it impossible for a credible socialist perspective to emerge. The shift towards the ideology of American-style consensus reinforces this possible disastrous evolution, which would impose apartheid at the world level. While the danger of this possibility should not be underestimated, there is one reason why it is not inevitable. The oligarchic centralisation of capital and its mode of managing the crisis of senile capitalism is committing itself to a general evolution towards the destruction of the whole future of humanity and perhaps life on the planet. An awareness of this perspective is growing. Will it enable the constitution of an alternative anti-oligarchy bloc? Would the emergence of such a bloc be facilitated by the degradation of the living conditions of the popular classes and large sections of the middle classes that this crisis will almost certainly produce? Here we see the importance of representations. Will these succeed in giving credibility to fascist-leaning responses ('it's the fault of the immigrants', of 'international terrorism')? Or will they fail to do so?

In the peripheries, the emergence of alternative national blocs (anti-imperialist), popular (anti-feudal, anti-comprador) and democratic, are coming up against visible difficulties. The nostalgic drifts – manipulated by imperialism and the local neo-compradors – are far from losing their strength. There, too, battles on ideological fronts, the dissection of discourse, are most necessary.

Beyond the analysis of the realities concerning both the popular and middle classes, can a concept of 'people' help us to develop strategies for the construction of a socialist convergence?

7 BEING MARXIST, BEING COMMUNIST, BEING INTERNATIONALIST

I would say that it is important to do politics (in the good sense of the term). The people in question is not defined in advance; this can only be done in its relation to both the immediate and more distinct objectives of the strategy to fight for the opening up of the socialist path. An anti-oligarchy people in the North? An anti-imperialist people in the South? This reality has previously existed, in moments of radicalisation of the struggle for national liberation and socialism. In Vietnam it became the active subject of history. This was indeed the case of a people who came together, but excluded the feudal and comprador classes.

The political classes

A concrete analysis of the conditions for struggling for the alternative with a socialist perspective should give special attention to the social groups that are particularly active. These are what are (inappropriately) called the 'political classes'.

Here we get into a jungle of entanglements which can only be disentangled one by one. I have tried to do it only for a few countries in the Bandung era.

The temptation has always been very great to replace the analysis of representations and the real choices of action by a general discourse on the petty bourgeoisie. It tends to be forgotten that this term does not usually constitute a very definite class, defined by objective criteria of status in the production system. The term was introduced by popular revolutionary talk of the 19th century and by Marx to identify more an attitude than a class. Its usage was always pejorative, if not sarcastic. The 'petty bourgeois' is an individual who is not bourgeois (they do not have access to capital, even at a modest level), but they believe themselves to be so.

The petty bourgeois way of thinking, widespread since then, is not reserved to one or several particular middle classes. One can see this in the conclusions to the representations that bombard them. Thus there is frequent abuse in sticking the label on anyone who does not agree (with you, or with the party that claims to be hardened and revolutionary). These abuses are why this term is losing ground and has become suspect.

The language of capitalist reproduction

The fashion from across the Atlantic has replaced these concepts shaped by social struggles, which Marxism tried to systematise, with a new language of civil society, good governance, fight against poverty, social justice.

I suggested in Chapter 6 a radical critique of this 'newspeak' which expresses an ideology that has a very definite function that aims at restricting thinking to what is required by capitalist reproduction.

Towards a second wave of victorious anti-capitalist struggles?

I shall just recapitulate the most recent developments that I have put forward on these questions, emphasising the most essential of what I feel to be new ones.

The transition from world capitalism to world socialism cannot be envisaged other than in the form of successive waves of advances (followed by possible retreats, alas!) in the struggles for human emancipation, just as capitalism itself has been the product, not of a European miracle shaped in a brief period in the Amsterdam/London/Paris triangle, but of a succession of waves that took place in different geographical regions from the Ancient World and from China to the Europe of the Italian cities, not forgetting the Muslim Orient.

Historical capitalism, which was the product of the last European wave, imposed itself, thus destroying the possible shaping of other forms of capitalism based on historical cultures other than that of Atlantic Europe, in particular on that of Confucian China.

Bourgeois thought, which is by nature linear and Eurocentric, did not have the necessary intellectual tools to think beyond capitalism. Its only thinkable future for humanity was oriented to the catching up of the under-developed countries that were backward. It could not imagine a future except as an imitation of the capitalist model such as it existed in the developed centres. From Rostow to the emerging countries this bourgeois thesis remains unchanged. My criticism of this thesis was in advance of the times, written even before Rostow's book (published in 1960).

7 BEING MARXIST, BEING COMMUNIST, BEING INTERNATIONALIST

Historical Marxisms which are, in spite of everything, impregnated by the same reductionist and linear vision of history, only partially understood the size of the challenge, whatever the nuances.

I therefore regard the 20th century as that of a first wave. Great advances have been made in the centres, in the form of social-democratic management (not to be confused with social liberalism), together with a broadening of the democratisation of society (particularly the emergence of women onto the scene). Reactionary attempts to halt these advances (fascisms) were finally put to flight. Revolutions in the name of socialism, first in the Russian semi-periphery, then in the Chinese periphery (and in some other places) beyond doubt constituted the most radical advances of the century. The globalisation of the struggle for regaining independence by the peoples of Asia and Africa forced imperialism to adjust to a new multipolar system in the post-war period.

These advances veritably transformed the societies of the North and the South, of the West and the East at unprecedented rates and not necessarily for the worse, as liberal propaganda has it. But they were shot through with contradictions and reached limits that prepared the way for later retreats from their first victories. I will not return to describing these ebbs and flows but just outline what seems to me to be their main origin and what the second wave of struggles should therefore put at the centre of their concerns.

First of all is the fascination with the state, not only of Leninism but also of social democracy and the national populisms of Bandung. The practice of democracy (when it existed) remained limited by the concept of progress from above, a fatal handicap for the socialisation of economic management.

Then there is also the underestimation – which is the least one can say – of the extent of the challenge created by the depth of the centre–periphery split. There are of course nuances on this issue too. From Baku, in 1920, Lenin foresaw that the revolutionary anti-capitalist movement was moving eastwards. But above all, the decisive contribution of Maoism finds its place here. Mao's agenda was to conceive the revolution as national (anti-imperialist), popular and democratic (anti-feudal, anti-comprador), opening the way to a very long, possible transition to socialism.

So, what are the conditions for the emergence of a second wave, 'the socialisms of the 21st century?

At the heart of the challenge lies the question of democracy and of the reconstruction of the world system.

The question of democracy

I start from the critique that Marx addressed to the bourgeois system as a whole.

Marx's instrument for analysing it is his theory of representation. Human beings not only live in a system (a historical social formation) but also in the way it is represented (by their ideology), which itself is ordered by the objective formation in which they live. It was religious (I call it 'metaphysical') in the ancient systems and economic (I call it 'economicist') under capitalism. I will not repeat all that I have already written about the contrast between the two. 'Representation' distinguishes human societies from animal societies: it governs the action strategies of the subjects of history, classes and nations.

In capitalism, religion, law and money constitute the three faces of the alienated representation of the capitalist reality, as Garo points out. As I have written, these three are inseparable: 'moneytheism' substitutes (or accompanies) monotheism.

But law, too, which becomes the foundation of the new state, perhaps democratic, is itself actively involved in the economic alienation. It transforms itself, from having been at the service of power (in the *anciens régimes*), to that of property. The democratic conquests have reached the limit that they cannot cross without getting out of capitalism. The bourgeois democracy is itself an alienated democracy. It forbids the crossing of the red line of sacrosanct property ownership. Law and money are thus inseparable. And this association accompanies the separation between the political management of society by electoral and multiparty representative democracy (where it exists) and the management of the economy which is abandoned to reason, attributed to the market. In politics citizens are equal before the law. In social reality, dominant and dominated, exploiters and exploited, are no longer equal in their capacity to make use of their rights. Social progress is exteriorised, it is not a constitutive part of the foundation of law and democracy.

7 BEING MARXIST, BEING COMMUNIST, BEING INTERNATIONALIST

The struggle for bourgeois democracy is perfectly justified in situations where it does not exist. One can understand the legitimacy of its claim to implement fundamental rights (of freedom of opinion, organisation, struggle, etc). Progress in this democratic field favours the development of struggles and a correct representation of the challenges. But this struggle in no way resolves the problem. The real challenge demands the invention of a law and a democracy that associates the freedom of individuals with social progress. This cannot be done without dethroning money, that is, extricating ourselves from capitalism.

Rather than discuss democracy (which always implies bourgeois democracy) one must discuss democratisation (considered as an endless process), synonym of the emancipation of individuals and peoples.

The second wave will not constitute progress compared with the first wave, if it does not make real progress in this direction.

To make progress in democratisation is impossible without bringing together what I call the 'social base' (social constituency) as opposed to the 'electoral base' (electoral constituency) in struggles that are convergent in diversity.

The social base exists objectively and brings together the immense majority of people both in the North and in the South because their adversary is always this same oligarchy that governs contemporary capitalism. Yet it is difficult to pass from an existence in itself to an existence for itself, defining the new subjects of transformation. It involves the formulation, groping, slow and difficult, of effective strategies. There is no alternative for the struggles conducted in this spirit with this objective.

The electoral base of the existing left groupings (where they exist) is, by nature, volatile because it functions within the limits of bourgeois democracy. The Leninist altercation – 'the parliamentarian cretinism' – is as vigorous as ever, confirmed each day by electoral disappointments.

A first question: is the prospect of emancipation as proposed above possible (critical utopia) or is it utopian in the common use of the term – a dream without any real possibility of fulfilment?

Is emancipation then really possible? The question often posed here is that of overcoming alienations. I mean by alienation the behaviour of human beings that attributes to forces outside themselves the obligation to act as they do. The most obvious case is the economistic alienation produced by the domination of capital (beyond the market) which imposes its needs like a force of nature outside the society, while the economy in question only exists through the social relationships that define its framework. My reading of Marx's *Capital: Critique of the Political Economy* is based on the central position of alienation.

But what are the other forms of alienation? Such as those that define religious beliefs? In general, is alienation not a condition that defines a human being? It is clear that if the reply to this question is that alienation is inherent in the human being, then the possibilities of freedom through the democratic management of the economy and of power are, by definition, limited. But what are those limits?

I therefore propose to distinguish the forms of alienation that I describe as social and which can therefore be situated in time and space, particular to a concrete society at a concrete moment of its history, like the economistic alienation that is peculiar to capitalism, or the religious alienations as they are experienced by the societies concerned, from those that would be anthropological (or, in my vocabulary, supra-historical). And on that basis I would be satisfied with defining the emancipation offered by the communist perspective as liberation from the social alienations alone. One can then give a more precise definition of the institutional forms of the management of the economy and of politics that facilitate progress in that direction.

The critical utopia comes within this framework and its limitations. I understand, by critical utopia, a vision of the future that is, in the end, much more realistic than its adversaries imagine. Even modest advance in that direction would produce a strong mobilisation of forces prepared to go still further. To renounce the critical utopia, when all is said and done, is to accept the barbarous drift of capitalism. I refuse this call for so-called realism, which is, in fact, submission to a reality that is itself only ephemeral.

Emancipation, a synonym for democratisation without limits: must it therefore eliminate the terms of alienation (religion, law and democracy, money) as they figure in the ideologies of anar-

7 BEING MARXIST, BEING COMMUNIST, BEING INTERNATIONALIST

chist and communist atheism? Or work out ways to control them: radical secularism, social democracy, the socialisation of economic management? I would opt for this second, modest interpretation for the long term of the communism of the future.

The peoples in question, do they want the democratisation as proposed above? Do they even want the limited democracy that is offered to them? This is where the representations come in, those produced by the system in which they live, the limits of action that they believe to be possible. In other words, it is a question of having a 'lucid consciousness' (or of their illusions to that effect), moving from the consciousness of oneself to the consciousness for oneself of the dominated classes.

Right now, the demand for democracy is not obvious. People are victims both of the ideological alienations specific to capitalism and of the immediate challenges of living (or even of surviving). They are not necessarily convinced that anything other than a daily adjustment and manoeuvre is possible.

In the centres the damages of alienation are visible. Do the young (and others!) want anything else than more of the same, to possess what they don't have and what others do have? The fact that they also want less inequality, more solidarity, does not fundamentally change the facts of this form of depoliticisation.

In the peripheries, living – often the same thing as surviving – understandably gives priority to eating, but also to having schools for children so that they have a chance to rise in the system, such as it is. This second form of depoliticisation is no less visible than the preceding one.

What, therefore, would be an effective way of dealing with this challenge?

The theory/practice dialectic cannot be ignored. Correct theory proceeds from an analysis of the reality; the rightness of the proposals that stem from it is then tested by action. The theoretical elaboration is never a spontaneous result of the movement, despite what certain people say. It needs 'theoreticians' (a term that is too academic and therefore pretentious), who are of the 'avant-garde' (a term that irritates because it reminds people of the way it was used by those who proclaimed themselves as such), and 'elites' (a term that is refused because it is the one that the ideology of the system used to designate those who are its servants). The Russian word 'intelligentsia' is no doubt the most appropriate.

Theory and practice are inseparable. There will be no movement towards democratic and social progress without formulating a programme that constructs convergence in diversity. Its definition cannot be avoided. I sum it up in one phrase: 'socialising economic management'.

In the centres, the operation cannot be initiated without first expropriating the oligarchy. It is not only in Russia that the oligarchy dominates the system, as I have said, it dominates just as much in the United States, in Europe and in Japan. Nationalisation (perhaps through the state) constitutes a first, essential measure. It is a long route, built up along the way, that has to be invented.

In the peripheries the national, popular and democratic programme contains its internal contradictions. Not only because its social base is composed of social sectors whose interests do not always converge. But also and as much because the historical task here is double and conflictual. It is necessary to catch up in the sense of developing productive forces (and there is a great temptation to take the formulas for doing so from capitalism), as this is necessary to leave poverty behind. And it is also necessary to do something else, to initiate social relationships based on solidarity instead of competition. The Russian and Chinese revolutions did this very vigorously in their early, victorious phases but then they gradually regressed and got bogged down in just catching up. It is a decisive lesson to draw from the first wave: to avoid getting mired in this contradiction must be a central aim of the concerns of the second wave.

It goes without saying that the successive phases of the long national, popular and democratic transition are based on conflictual compromises that oppose aspirations to socialism against forces that have a capitalist orientation. I refer again here to the experience of Maoism and the powerful analysis made of it by Lin Chun. On the positive side there was the invention of the 'mass line'. What eventually destroyed it was the lack of institutions guaranteeing rights (including of the individual) and justice. We could also refer to the proposals and experiences of worker self-management, of participatory democracy and others. They should be read and re-read with a critical mind.

Recourse to the instrument of an enlightened despotism is nevertheless sometimes inevitable. Forcing recalcitrant fathers to send their daughters to school: is this an antidemocratic procedure or the only way to open the path to democratisation?

I analysed, in Chapter 4, some of these advances during our era (in Afghanistan and so-called communist Yemen).

The new economics cannot be reduced to the socialisation of its management. It must integrate the society/nature relationship and redefine the development of the productive forces, taking into account this relationship. The destructive dimension of accumulation is now very much greater than its constructive dimension. Pursued in the forms that capitalism gives it means destroying the individual, nature and whole peoples. Socialism is not 'capitalism without capitalists'. The 'solar socialism' of Altvater is relevant here and is convincing in my opinion.

The question of globalisation

I shall be brief here because I have written much on the subject. I shall just retrace the essential of the conclusions.

Liberal globalisation wants to build another world which is in the process of emerging, based on an apartheid at the world level, still more barbaric than what we have experienced since the end of the Second World War. The policies being implemented by the powers, who are in desperate straits, in response to the financial crisis are exclusively aimed at restoring the liberal world order. As in 1920, it is an effort to return to the belle époque. And it is certain that there will be the same threat of new collapses of the system, still more serious.

This pursuit, against all odds, by the oligarchy of the imperialist Triad to continue their domination over the world system involves the recourse to permanent, armed violence through the military control of the planet. As long as this project is not completely defeated, all advances anywhere will be extremely vulnerable. Constructing convergence in the diversity of struggles must give a central place in its strategies to the objective of routing the militarisation of the world. I have been insisting on this point since 1990, even before the emergence of the Social Forums.

A Bandung 2, the Bandung of the peoples (but also with the necessary and possible perspective of the Bandung of the states) would be an excellent way of terminating both the military interventions of the collective imperialism of the Triad and the implementation of a restored liberal globalisation.

From Marx to historical Marxism

As we know, Marx used to say he was not a Marxist as soon as he saw the dangers of the historical Marxisms of the parties that claimed his thinking.

It is not the place to develop a critique of historical Marxism here, even a rapid one. I should just like to mention the five fields of questions that, I believe, cannot be avoided when one declares oneself Marxist. Not in the sense of adhering to the historical Marxisms of the past, but in the spirit of starting from Marx.

The question of the articulation of instances (base and superstructure, economics, politics, ideology and culture), to use our well-known jargon, has given rise to a drift to which I feel it is necessary to respond.

Marx seems to me to have established very well that the base (the organisation of production and work) was always determinant in the last instance. It was so at the dawn of the development of the productive forces in the communitarian systems (communal formations governed by the ideology of family or kinship), relationships that managed the birth of social classes; it was also the case in the long period of the tributary systems of premodern classes; and, of course, under capitalism.

But Marx took the precaution of articulating the political and ideological superstructure on this base in a way that was specific to capitalism – different from previous systems. In our jargon (that I share with others), the economic base does not become dominant, or directly dominant, except under capitalism. In the previous systems, it was the political power that constituted the directly dominant authority. I have summed up this reversal in this sentence: in capitalism wealth is the source of power, in

7 BEING MARXIST, BEING COMMUNIST, BEING INTERNATIONALIST

the previous systems it was the contrary. The dominant political power needed an ideology that suited its reproduction – the state religion; that of capital was economicism – commodity alienation.

But in all cases it is necessary to make explicit how these articulations function. Marx did not propose a general theory (inevitably transhistoric), because his method forbade him to do so. He therefore contented himself with analysing concretely how these articulations worked in various places and times. Whether these analyses were later confirmed or invalidated does not concern me.

In contrast, historical Marxisms proposed this general theory, declaring that the different instances were always and necessarily constituted in the same way. This general theory was taken to an extreme by Althusser with his concept of 'over-determination'.

My criticism of this shift of historical Marxism towards a kind of historical determinism led me to propose instead a concept of under-determination. I mean that the different instances are ordered, not exclusively by the requirements of a global consistency but equally by internal logics of their own. The case of religious logics could, I thought, give us some striking examples in this field. More important is what I derived from my concept of under-determination: that the conflict of the instances can end up in a positive revolutionary change, but it can also lead the society into an impasse, if not regression. Revolution and chaos are both different and possible outcomes from these conflicts. Therefore importance must be given, in analysing these representations, to these questions of internal logics specific to the different fragments of the social reality.

Over-determination proved to be an encouragement of a simplifying drift which was perhaps dominant in popularised Marxism.

This consisted of the false theory of the ideology as a reflection, that is, it directly expressed the requirements of the reproduction of the economic base. Marx used the term reflection here and there but, it seems to me, in order to characterise these extreme cases when the ideology becomes purely functional. This is what, in my opinion, transmitted the liberal virus. But it is far from being the rule that governs the relationship between the instances.

Perhaps the authorities of historical Marxism were aware that this simplification did not always help to progress in analysing reality and they resorted to a rather vague phrase 'the autonomy of the instances'. Is this an escape when confronted by a real difficulty? What is the exact meaning and content of this autonomy? Is it only passing resistance, submitting to the requirements of the base and ending by withering away? This is probably the meaning that it has been given. I suggest going much further.

The modern state, which is capitalist, would not exist if it were not strongly linked to the requirements of capitalist domination and reproduction. This was said by Marx and I agree.

But from there to conclude that the state, because it has never been other than a class state and cannot be otherwise and therefore it should disappear in the classless society, seems to me to be a problem. Marx and Engels sometimes implied this quick conclusion, sometimes something else: that the proletariat could not take over the bourgeois state to put it at their own service, so it was necessary to destroy it. And replace it by another state, 'the administration of things and no longer the government of men', as the utopian socialists defined it, and Marx took up the formula. I have reached a somewhat different proposal: of the state as organiser and socialiser of the management of advanced and complex systems of production. And with this in mind I place culture (communist culture, much more than an ideology) in the command position, culture so defined becoming the new dominant instance.

But the simplifying drift was greatly to obscure an analysis of the requirements of the state in a transition period. And while one admits that it will be a long transition (a secular one) the question acquires a central importance. It does not only concern the national, popular, democratic state of the long transition based on the revolutionary advances in the peripheries of the system. It concerns every state in their no shorter transition in the developed centres. It requires the articulation between the needs for the socialisation of economic management and those for the progress in the democratisation of society. It requires the articulation between the policies of (national) states and the implementation of a multipolar globalisation.

7 BEING MARXIST, BEING COMMUNIST, BEING INTERNATIONALIST

I think that this last dimension of actually existing capitalism, the imperialist and polarising globalisation that underlies its expansion, has been – and it is the least one could say – underestimated by historical Marxisms both as to its reality and in the consequences that it brought about.

I won't come back to this question, quite simply because it is around this that all my reflections and proposals (or almost all) have revolved for the past fifty years.

Marx did not produce a general theory of society. It was not even a general theory of history – he was careful to avoid this.

Does this mean that reflection, not 'beyond' Marx (which would imply a fundamental revision of Marx's propositions), but 'outside' Marx, in the field of anthropology, are forbidden?

I think it would be pointless to say so.

For my part I have dared (without having any qualification for arrogating to myself the right to do so) to propose some thoughts concerning the pyramid of alienations that do in fact stand out in Marx's views in this field.

I think that a reflection of the same kind on the question of power would not be without interest, among other things in order to be able to understand its representations better, both the scientific and the distortions. Militants know the problem through their practice. They know how to distinguish the logic of organisation from the logic of struggles. Anthropologists, philosophers and, in particular, psychoanalysts have posed the question of a human being's requirement for democracy and also for expressing power. I do not believe that Marxism requires one to ignore these issues.

Marx believed he had detected the aspiration to communism in the real movement of society. This is the reason why he mistrusted its mutation into a project of a political, utopian or so-called realist organisation. Marx left the class in its ensemble – the general proletariat – to invent its route to communism.

I rallied to this thesis which assumes, in its way, an optimistic vision of human reason. Other thinkers outside Marx (and not starting from Marx) do not share this vision. Freud is an example. In spite of the real greatness of this thinker, his theses do not convince me because, by reading them and discovering the representation of the world that he proposes (as Marx did for all the thinkers), one cannot, in my humble opinion, avoid finding the representations of the Viennese bourgeois in crisis.

I also tried to read Keynes in the same way, which was that of Marx. Keynes is not just an economist. He is an economist, of course, and even a great one. But he was great because he was not only an economist, he was a thinker. Gilles Dostaler and Bernard Maris in *Capitalisme et Pulsion de Mort* understood this and their book was recently presented in this spirit.

Keynes's vision of the future of humanity was optimistic. He saw that the level of development of the productive forces that had been acquired enabled humanity to emancipate itself from the economic question (in his beautiful speeches to our great grandchildren). A society that was freed from the chains of obligatory work was therefore possible: a society that passed its time cultivating human relationships, a society that was truly emancipated and cultivated. This objective, in its way, is none other than that of Marx's communism. It is the reason why capitalism is a system that is now obsolescent, whose time is now over. The thinking of Keynes constitutes, I believe, one of the examples that prove the rightness of Marx's vision: humanity aspires to communism. Not only its popular classes (whom Keynes distrusted), but even its greatest thinkers. Keynes was certainly not the first one to have conceived this radiant future. Before him, the utopians had done so.

However the equally necessary reading of Keynes the economist is, in my view, disappointing. Of course Keynes was far above the conventional vulgar economists of his day (and their descendants, the pure economists of today). And his proposals constitute an approach to reality infinitely more powerful than those of our miserable liberals. But the concepts that he advocated to grasp the economic reality in a different way (the preference for liquidity in particular) are not free from the empirical and direct observation of the phenomena. Marx goes much further: the preference for liquidity that Keynes rightly associated with the worship of money expressed the commodity alienation, which is fundamental for the reproduction of the system.

Keynes thus took no notice of the tendency to pauperisation that is necessarily produced by the logic of accumulation. The

7 BEING MARXIST, BEING COMMUNIST, BEING INTERNATIONALIST

effect of this tendency was not in fact very visible in the England of his time. Nevertheless it was very much present in the British empire, as the South African communist party wrote at the time. But Keynes was not concerned about it.

As a thinker, a utopian communist, Keynes was certainly a very sensitive person. But he remained a prisoner of the prejudices of his class. His scorn for the popular classes, incapable, according to him, of fighting for this radiant future to which he and his Bloomsbury friends aspired, betrayed the education that he had received. Rather like the 'bobos' (see Translator's note) of Paris today, he thought that the task of changing the world was the exclusive domain of the elites.

There is no doubt that the observations of Keynes about the British workers of his period (and our own) are quite perceptive. But to understand this, it is necessary to leave behind the viewpoint of the popular classes in the rich centres alone, to see the reality of the globalised capitalist system. Imperialist rent explains this kind of behaviour in Britain. Looking at the world system as a whole thus means departing from Marx and posing the questioning of capitalism in other terms. It means giving all due importance to the struggles for emancipation of the peoples in the peripheries, of which Keynes had no idea.

Can social movements measure up to the challenge?

Here, too, I shall be brief and just refer to my conclusions.

The progressive social movements, because they are still very fragmented and in defensive positions, are in danger of being dragged down, even retreating, to the benefit of the reactionary movements based on para-religious, para-ethnic, para-populist and other illusions. There is no lack of examples of political religions, of new sects, of ethnocracies.

In these conditions, it is important to distinguish the possible collapses of the system caused by the sharpening of its own internal contradictions on the one hand, from the retreats of the system under the blows of lucid popular and democratic advances on the other hand. Because of this I have suggested describing certain transitions in the past (for example from the Roman Empire to

European feudalism) as the path to decadence as opposed to the revolutionary path which is characterised by the transitions to historical capitalism and socialism: 'revolution or decadence' (my version) 'socialism or barbarism' (Rosa Luxemburg's), or again, 'lucid transition or chaos' (my recent expression in response to the ongoing crisis) – these are all synonymous. Up until now the world is more engaged on the road to chaos because the movements in struggle have not measured up to the challenge.

For this reason, enormous importance must be given to the ideological battle. I should mention here the critiques that I have made of the post-modern discourse of Negri in particular. There are idiocies like 'cognitive capitalism', or the 'death of Marx', the retreat to the bourgeois ideology of the freedom of the individual, which has already become 'the subject of history' (as Habermas puts it), technologism (the essence of the challenges and transformations under way being attributed to the technological revolution), the elimination of the essential reality of contemporary capitalism (the domination of the oligarchy), if not naive formulas (horizontal communication replacing vertical hierarchies). All these delay the development of a lucid awareness of the real challenges, in the short and the long term, of the casualisation of labour and the increased subordination of the peoples of the South to work and wars.

References

It was not my intention to retrace the phases of the formation of concepts and conclusions that are presented here. I shall just briefly indicate the texts of mine that could help the reader to discover their development, presented chronologically.

Accumulation on a World Scale (2 vols) (1972) New York, Monthly Review Press

The Law of Value and Historical Materialism (1978) New York, Monthly Review Press. A new edition is in preparation.

Class and Nation, Historically and in the Current Crisis (1980) New York, Monthly Review Press
- Communal formations, Chapter 2
- Tributary formations, Chapter 3
- Revolution or decadence, Conclusion

Eurocentrism (2010) 2nd edition, Oxford and New York, Pambazuka Press

7 BEING MARXIST, BEING COMMUNIST, BEING INTERNATIONALIST

and Monthly Review Press
Spectres of Capitalism, a Critique of Current Intellectual Fashions (1998) New York, Monthly Review Press
- Unity and changes in the ideology of political economy, Chapter 2
- Overdetermination and underdetermination in history, Chapter 3
- The withering away of the law of value, Chapter 5
- Pure economics, the contemporary world's witchcraft, Chapter 8

Obsolescent Capitalism (2003) London, Zed Books
- The political economy of the 20th century, Chapter 1
- Historical Marxism and historical Keynesianism, Chapter 2
- Socialisation through the market or socialisation through democratisation, Chapter 2
- Financialisation, a temporary phenomenon?, Chapter 3
- The collective imperialism of the Triad, Chapter 4

The Liberal Virus, Permanent War and the Americanization of the World (2004) New York, Monthly Review Press
- Pauperisation and global polarisation, Chapter 3
- The ideology of modernity, Chapter 4

Beyond US Hegemony? Assessing the Prospects for a Multipolar World (2006) London, Zed Books
- The drama of great revolutions, Appendix 1
- The weight of imperialism, Appendix 1

The World We Wish to See: Revolutionary Objectives in the 21st Century (2008) New York, Monthly Review Press

From Capitalism to Civilization (2010) Delhi, Tulika Books
- The contribution of Maoism, pp. 33–36
- Formal logics or materialist dialectics, pp. 52–57
- Productivity of social labour, pp. 57–67
- From the law of value to globalised value, pp. 67–69 (see also new edition of *The Law of Value and Historical Materialism* above)
- Market economics or capitalism of the oligopolies? Chapter 4
- The 'multitude', critique of the concept, Annex 2, p. 147 onwards
- On the cultural front, full speed backwards, Annex 2, p. 151 onwards
- No authentic democracy without social progress, Annex 3, p. 157 onwards

L'Éveil du Sud (2008) Paris, Le Temps des Cerises

Other references

Altvater, Elmar (2009) 'Energy crisis, climate change collapse, hunger and financial instabilities: the plagues of capitalism', 12 February, www.oid-ido.org/article.php3?id_article=730, accessed 29 June 2010

Amin, Samir (1976) *Unequal Development*, New York, Monthly Review Press

Amin, Samir (2001) 'Marx et la démocratie', *La Pensée*, no. 328

Amin, Samir (2004) 'Cinquante ans après Bandoung', *Recherches Internationales* vol. 73, no. 4

Amin, Samir (2005) 'Empire et multitude', *La Pensée*, no. 343

Amin, Samir and Frank, André Gunder (1981) *Let's Not Wait for 1984*, New York, Monthly Review Press
Dostaler, Gilles and Maris, Bernard (2009) *Capitalisme et Pulsion de Mort*, Paris, Albin Michel
Etiemble, René (1988) *L'Europe chinoise*, Paris, Gallimard
Garo, Isabelle (2000) *Marx, Une Critique de la Philosophie*, Paris, Seuil
Mannheim, Karl (1952 [1985]) *Ideology and Utopia*, Mariner

Index

accumulation, by dispossession 1–3, 35, 52–5
Afghanistan, communism 82–90, 93
Africa
    agrarian reform 118, 119–20
    development aid 136–7
    dispossession 53
    food security 107–8
    land tenure 114–15
African Command 35
agrarian reform 117–25
agriculture
    capitalist modernisation 105–6, 125–7
    family agriculture 101–4
    peasant agriculture 104–5
aid, development aid 130–45
alienation 73, 152, 180–3
alternative world movement 27, 125
Altvater, Elmar 29, 38, 185
Amerindians, dispossession 53
Ancien Régime 55, 58, 74, 75, 147, 167–8
apartheid at world level 6, 8, 27, 63, 147, 161, 176, 185
Aron, Raymond 153, 157
Arrighi, Giovanni 6

Bagchi, Amiya Kumar 54
Bandung period 16, 18, 60, 65, 82–3, 94, 138, 186
belle époque
    first (1890–1914) 4, 168–9
    second (1990–2008) 5, 169
Berthelot, Jacques 124
bobos (bohemian bourgeois) 76, 191
Boris, Jean-Pierre 125
bourgeois civilisation, end of 69–70
bourgeois democracy 14, 162–4, 180–1

Brazil 64
Brown, Gordon 11
Brunel, Sylvie 107
Burkina Faso 121
Bush, George W. 13, 34

Cabral, Amilcar 121
capitalism
    agricultural modernisation 105–6, 125–7
    decline 60–2
    ending 7–8, 16–17
    globalisation 70–3
    historical development 40–50, 51–77, 178
    history of crisis 3–7, 21–38
    neoliberal phase 9–10, 159–62
    phases 167–9
    polarisation 62, 71–3
    post-war growth 21–2
    reality 153–8
    senile 69–70, 77
    socialism transition 2, 8, 27–8, 36, 60–1, 64–7, 178–80
    centre–periphery conflict 64–7, 160, 179
    see also North–South conflict
China
    Confucianism 150
    global strategy 12–13
    historical development 40–50
    land tenure 115–17
    revolution 66, 79–82, 91–2, 184
civil society, concept 133–5
class, and struggle 174–7
climate change 139
Clinton, Bill 34
Colombia 95
colonialism 4, 53–5

communism
  meaning of 146–7
  modern societies 83–94
  Nepal 94–9
  revolutions 66–7
comprador state 163–4
Comte, Auguste 40, 74
Confucianism 150
consensus, political 14
Cuba 59, 66, 78, 91, 103, 138, 144, 164
customary management, land tenure 112–15

debts, development aid 140
delinking 36, 58, 72, 130
democracy
  bourgeois democracy 14, 162–4, 180–1
  Nepal 96–7
  socialist 90–3
democratisation 181–5
development, principles 141–5
development aid 130–45
Development Cooperation Forum (DCF) 140
Dostaler, Gilles 190

ecological movement 10
Egypt 87, 88
emancipation 8–11, 74–5, 152, 181–2
energy crisis 2–3, 25
Enlightenment 48–9, 73–4, 93, 129
Europe
  Americanisation 161–2
  colonialism 53–5
  feudalism 110–11
  historical development 40–50
European Union (EU) 37, 62, 107

family agriculture 101–4
feudalism, Europe 110–11

financial crisis (2008) 3–7, 21–38, 169
financialisation 28–32
food crisis 25
food sovereignty 107–8
Fourth International 67
France
  agriculture 102
  Marx's critique of 157–8
Frank, André Gunder 6, 7, 23, 175
French Revolution 55, 58, 75, 91, 129, 157–8
Freud, Sigmund 189–90

G7/G8 62, 131–2
G20 summit (2009) 11–13
Gaddafi, Muammar 87, 89
Galbraith, John Kenneth 22
Garo, Isabelle 147, 148–9, 153, 155, 180
geo-economy, Africa 136–7
geopolitics, capitalism crisis 166–7
globalisation
  capitalism 70–3
  historical 44–6
  oligarchies 8–13, 68–70, 185–6
  struggle against 27–8
governance, concept 135
Gowan, Peter 29
Gramsci, Antonio 14, 59, 167–8
Green Revolution 104, 105
Guinea-Bissau 121

Haiti 143
historical development, societies 40–50
Hu Jintao 12
humanitarianism 129–45

imperialism, Triad (United States, Europe, Japan) 6–7, 13–14, 26, 62, 159, 169, 185–6
imperialist rent 1–3, 35, 130, 163

INDEX

India 54, 64, 98–9, 113
Industrial Revolution 54–5, 58
internationalism, meaning of 146–7
International Monetary Fund (IMF) 31, 62, 142
International Workers Association 129
Iraq, communism 82–90

Kassem, Abdel Karim 86
Kautsky, Karl 103, 119
Keynes, John Maynard 1, 4, 10, 156, 190–1
Kondratieff cycles 167

land reform
    peasantry role 117–22
    state role 122–5
land tenure 109–17
    customary management 112–15
    private ownership 110–12
language, development of 46–7
latifundia 103, 104, 114
Latin America
    agriculture 103–4
    socialism 93–4
Lenin, V.I. 4, 79, 119, 168, 179
liberal virus 14, 159–62
Lin Chun 92, 184
Lordon, Frédéric 29
Losurdo, Domenico 61
lucidity 73–7
Luxemburg, Rosa 77, 192

Machiavelli, Niccolo 158
Madagascar 137
Mali 121
Mannheim, Karl 152
Maoism 79–82, 179, 184
    Nepal 94–9
Maris, Bernard 190
market economy, collapse 28–9

Marx, Karl
    Capital 153–4
    capitalist reality critique 153–8
    social thought critique 149–52
Marxism
    consumption ideology 15
    generalism 40–1
    historical 72, 129–30, 164–5, 186–91
    meaning of 146–58
    renewal 18
    terminology 172–8
materialist dialectic 151
mercantilism 55, 57–8, 71
Merkel, Angela 11
migrants, land rights 123
militarisation 34–5
Mill, John Stuart 1
monopoly rent 2, 20n1
Morin, François 29
Muslim Brotherhood 87, 88, 89

Nasser, Gamal Abdel 87, 89
natural resources
    access to 26, 33, 137
    exploitation 57
Nazism 15, 32
Negri, Antonio 192
neoliberalism 23–5, 159–62
neo-Marxism 146
Nepal, Maoism 94–9
New Deal 15, 32, 157
Niger 136–7
Nimeiry, General 87, 89
Non-Aligned Movement 144
non-governmental organisations (NGOs) 134–5
North, agriculture 101–4
North Atlantic Treaty Organisation (NATO) 11–13, 35, 62
North–South conflict 32–8, 64–7
    see also centre–periphery

Obama, Barack 11, 13, 34
obscurantism 76
oligarchies 8–13, 68–70, 160, 184
    see also Triad
oligopolies
    capitalism crisis 5–7, 17, 26, 32
    financialisation 28–32
Organisation for Economic Cooperation and Development (OECD) 62, 107, 108, 131, 140
over-determination 187

Paris Declaration on Aid Effectiveness 131–3
Parmentier, Bruno 108
pauperisation, by accumulation 1–3
peasantry
    agriculture 104–5
    and class 175–6
    dispossession 1–3, 52–5
    land tenure 109–17
    mobilisation 126–7
    Nepal 95–6
peripheries
    revolutions 59–64
    see also centre–periphery conflict
petty bourgeois 177
polarisation, capitalism 62, 71–3
political classes 177
political conflicts 170–2
political economy, Marxian critique 153–7
popular fronts 15, 32
proletarianisation 165, 173
proletariat, terminology 173–4

Rawls, John 133
Reagan, Ronald 23, 131
reality
    capitalist 153–8
    representations 150–2
regionalisation 37
    premodern 44–6

religions, as representations 149–50
representation, Marxist theory 149–52, 180
revolutions 66–7, 75, 78–99, 179
Rostow, W. W. 178
Russia, agrarian reform 118–19
Russian Revolution 79, 88, 91, 184

Sarkozy, Nicolas 11, 13
Second International 78–9, 164
Sen, Amartya 9, 133
Senegal 115
Shanghai Cooperation Organization (SCO) 13
slave trade 53
social imperialism 129–30, 163
socialism
    existing 22
    first wave 18, 21, 32, 59–64, 179
    revolutions 78–99, 179
    second wave 178–80
    transition from capitalism 2, 8, 27–8, 36, 60–1, 64–7, 178–80
social justice, concept 133
social movements 191–2
social struggles 170–2
societies, historical development 40–50
solar socialism 38, 185
South
    agriculture 104–5
    awakening 16, 59–64, 162
    development aid 130–45
    see also North–South conflict
southern Africa, agriculture 103, 104
South–South cooperation 144–5
South Yemen, communism 82–90
Sovietism 78–9, 88
Soviet Union 32, 66
state
    imperialist 163–4
    land reform role 122–5
Stiglitz Commission 11–12

Stiglitz, Joseph 9, 133
Sudan, communism 82–90, 93
Supachai Panitchpakdi 12

Thatcher, Margaret 23
Third International 18, 82, 130, 164
Triad (United States, Europe, Japan)
    development aid 132–3
    geopolitics 138
    imperialism 6–7, 13–14, 26, 62, 159, 169, 185–6
    militarisation 34–5
tributary societies 41–6
Trotskyism 67

under-determination 150, 152, 187
United Arab Emirates 86
United Nations, Millennium Declaration 131–2
United Nations Conference on Trade and Development (UNCTAD) 12
United Nations Framework Convention on Climate Change (UNFCCC) 139
United States
    agriculture 102
    capitalism 161–2
    hegemony 11–13, 62
    see also Triad
universalism 76–7

Vietnam 56–7, 64, 66, 103, 115, 117, 177

Wallerstein, Immanuel 6
Wen Tiejun 46
wheeler-dealers 68–9
World Bank 62, 107
World Trade Organisation (WTO) 36, 62, 112, 124–5
writing, development of 46–7

Global History: a View from the South
Samir Amin

978-1-906387-96-9
2010
Paperback £14.95

Responding to the need to take a fresh look at world history, hitherto dominated by Eurocentric ideologues and historians in their attempt to justify the nature and character of modern capitalism, this book looks at the ancient world system and how it influenced the development of the modern world. It also analyses the origin and nature of modern globalisation and the challenges it presents in achieving socialism.

Amin, one of the best-known thinkers of his generation, examines a theme that has been primordial to his contribution to political and economic thought: the question of unequal development. This is a refreshing and creative work that is necessary reading for anyone wanting to understand the real process of history.

I always learn important things when I read Samir Amin. This book is no exception. It is full of original interpretations and is required reading for all who are seriously interested in global history.

Immanuel Wallerstein, Yale University

Order your copy from www.pambazukapress.org